THE SOUND OF BEAUTY

Michael Kurek

The Sound of Beauty

A Classical Composer on Music in the Spiritual Life

IGNATIUS PRESS   SAN FRANCISCO

Cover art:
Rose window, Cathedral of Our Lady of Strasbourg, France
Photograph by Clostridium, Wikimedia Commons

Cover design by Enrique J. Aguilar

© 2019 by Ignatius Press, San Francisco
Foreword © 2019 by Joseph Pearce
All rights reserved
ISBN 978-1-62164-271-8
Library of Congress Catalogue number 2019932522
Printed in the United States of America ∞

CONTENTS

ABOUT THE AUTHOR

Billboard chart-topping and award-winning classical composer Michael Kurek has established a reputation in the
world of symphonic and chamber music with concerts,
broadcasts, and digital streams of his music throughout the
United States and in sixty-one countries on six continents.
He also happens to be a certified catechist of the Catholic Church and an ardent promoter of truth, beauty, and
goodness in the arts. His numerous awards for composition
include the prestigious Academy Award in Music from the
American Academy of Arts and Letters (the Academy's
top annual award for lifetime achievement in composition, now called the Arts and Letters Award) and awards
from the League of American Orchestras, Broadcast Music
Inc. (BMI), National Endowment for the Arts (NEA),
Meet the Composer, Music Teachers National Association
(MTNA), and Tanglewood. He holds a doctorate in composition from the University of Michigan and serves on
the faculty of Vanderbilt University, where he chaired the
department of composition for fourteen years. His chart-
topping 2017 classical album, *The Sea Knows*, is available
on CD and in download formats wherever recordings are
sold. Free streaming music and more information about his
work can be found at www.michaelkurek.com.

FOREWORD

by Joseph Pearce

I first met Michael Kurek many years ago at a talk I was giving in Nashville. We struck up an instant friendship but did not meet each other again for several years. It was not until I became director of the Center for Faith and Culture at Aquinas College in Nashville that we really got to know each other. I often stayed with Michael and his wife Crystal, a very fine musical theater performer, during my monthly sojourns in Nashville. On many a joyful evening we waxed as the day waned, discussing Catholic culture in general, and music and literature in particular. It was such a privilege to be able to ask Michael all my inarticulately expressed questions on music. He was both maestro and mentor. His own compositions were a great inspiration, and his knowledge of music opened new vistas of aesthetic appreciation for me. I longed for others to have the opportunity to learn from him as I had done. I wanted others to gain the knowledge and understanding of music that Michael is uniquely able to offer, and more important, I wanted them to receive the wisdom he has accrued from a life of musical composition and the years spent as a professor of music at Vanderbilt University, all of which had been baptized by the deep Catholic faith to which he had returned after years as an Evangelical.

With the foregoing in mind, it will not surprise the reader that I am overjoyed that *The Sound of Beauty* is

being published. I know of no other book on music that
articulates the Catholic aesthetic so masterfully. This, in
itself, makes the present volume a precious jewel to be
cherished. And yet, as a rarity, it is never rarefied. It never
loses touch with the reader. On the contrary, Dr. Kurek
takes us by the hand and leads us through the physical
basics, explaining music in purely material terms. It is
only after we have mastered the physics of music that he
leads us into the metaphysics, showing us the goodness,
truth, and beauty of aural creation and aural creativity. He
shows us how great musical compositions can be considered "sculptures in sound", communicating to our sense
of hearing as Michelangelo's *Pietà* communicates to our
sense of sight. He also stresses the importance of narrative
in music, inviting analogies with literature. One thinks
perhaps of the story being told by Beethoven in his Sixth
Symphony and its evocation of a rural idyll, with wood-
wind instruments mimicking the song of the nightingale
and cuckoo; or one might be reminded of Schubert's
Piano Quintet in A Major and its suggestive aural allu-
sions to a trout swimming in a stream, or of Debussy's *La
mer* or Vaughan Williams' *The Lark Ascending*.

Such narrative can be found in Dr. Kurek's own inter-
nationally acclaimed compositions. In discussing the inspi-
rational and aspirational aspects of his Second Symphony,
he states that he hoped to create "a musical counterpart to
the allegories of J. R. R. Tolkien and C. S. Lewis in the
form of a purely musical 'fairy tale in sound' containing
hidden Christian symbolism".[1] He has written a ballet
based on Shakespeare's *Macbeth*, and the sleeve notes to

---

[1] "Symphony no. 2: Tales from the Realm of Faerie", *Faith and Culture*,
November 8, 2018, https://www.faithandculture.com/home/2018/11/8
-symphony-no-2. *See* Appendix F, p. 221.

his chart-topping CD *The Sea Knows* illustrate the visual nature of his musical sensibility. His *Serenade for Violoncello and Harp* is a love song, composed for his wife, in which the "long-breathed melodies" of the cello "seem to play the role of the lover singing under a balcony", as Taylor Jones puts it in the album's liner notes.[2] In *Savannah Shadows*, Dr. Kurek describes the "mysterious harmonies and long, exotic, drooping phrases" as "a kind of musical Spanish moss". In the "constantly evolving, descending melodic lines" of *Moon Canticle*, Dr. Kurek seeks to simulate "a continual shower of moonbeams falling upon an enchanted forest of shifting harmonic shadows". The literary connection is most manifest in the title track of the CD, "The Sea Knows", a wordless aural re-presentation of a short verse written by Dr. Kurek himself. The tone poem harmonizes with its literary namesake and illustrates it without language: "Like peeling back successive layers of an onion, the tonal structure of the work is carefully designed to reflect the poem as a process of self-discovery.... The cello's more discursive and overtly emotional part might represent the perspective of the person in the poem standing by the sea, while the lush richness of the full string section would seem to evoke the vastness and omniscience of the sea itself." In the musical composition, as in the poem, the sea serves as a metaphor for God, in whose presence the watcher at the ocean's edge is moved to contemplation.

It is this spirit of what might be called musical realism that animates Dr. Kurek's whole approach to "the sound of beauty". He sees music as a mainstay of human culture and as a manifestation of God's grandeur in the cosmos and in the

---

[2] Liner notes for Michael Kurek, *The Sea Knows*, with Ovidiu Marinescu, Soledad Yaya, the Atlantic Ensemble, Duo Portinari, and the Vanderbilt Strings, Navona NV6111, 2017, compact disc.

God-given creative gifts of those who compose, play, and listen to music. As a realist, both philosophically and musically, Dr. Kurek takes us beyond the relativism of those who believe that beauty is in the eye of the beholder to show us that it is in the thing beheld. He shows us how to avoid the relativist error of confusing and conflating goodness, truth, and beauty with preference, prejudice, and opinion.

Preference, which is often kindled by prejudice, has nothing to do with beauty. Many young people prefer rap to Rachmaninoff, but this says nothing about the relative merits of either form of "music". One likes rap not because of its beauty but because of its message, with the ugliness and brutality of the sound often unfortunately reflecting the ugliness and brutality of the message. By way of contrast, one *does* like Rachmaninoff because of its beauty, which is inseparable from our sense that it is also good and true. It violates our sense of reality to say that Rachmaninoff's *Rhapsody on a Theme of Paganini* is ugly or bad; it is clearly neither, whether we prefer it to other forms of music or not. There is something about what it is that transcends our opinions and prejudices.

Let us leave the final words to Dr. Kurek himself, discoursing on "the mystery and the wonder of the sanctified human imagination, be it in fairy tales or traditional classical music":

> Unlike, say, Narnia, with its specific allegory of Christ's redemptive work, purely instrumental music can be an allegorical narrative more generally—of purposefulness moving through time toward a goal; of love, sadness, struggle, hope, and ultimate victory.[3]

[3] Kurek, "Symphony no. 2". *See* Appendix F, p. 224.

INTRODUCTION

My reversion to the Catholic faith after many years as an Evangelical Protestant had a great deal to do with gaining a better understanding of the balance between the doctrines of *immanence* and *transcendence*. Immanence—not to be confused with imminence (the quality of being about to happen) or eminence (importance)—has to do with God's omnipresence in His creation. He is not only *in* everything but continues to sustain its existence and to hold together every atom of matter (Col 1:17). Pantheism might be considered an extreme distortion of immanence, where God is so much in everything as to be inseparable from it, so that the creation *is* God.

The doctrine of transcendence is the counterbalance to immanence, clarifying that the creation itself is not God. Although God is in His creation, He also transcends it. He is above and outside it too. He existed before creating anything, and even if He chose to destroy all creation, He would still exist. An extreme distortion of transcendence might be found in the classic heresies of Gnosticism and Manichaeism. Among other things, these heresies postulated a dualism, radically separating the spiritual and the material. This had the effect of denying or denigrating the physical/immanent world in favor of the spiritual/transcendent. In reply, Saint Irenaeus wrote in his treatise *Against Heresies* (ca. 180), "If the flesh may not be saved, of course neither did the Lord redeem us by his own blood."[1]

---

[1] Irenaeus, *Against Heresies*, trans. John Keble (Oxford: James Parker, 1872), 5.2.2, p. 452.

As a Protestant, I was personally a little out of balance, leaning too much toward the transcendent. I am not saying that this is what all of Protestantism intentionally teaches, because it was as a Protestant that I first learned these doctrines and heard that they should theoretically be in balance. But perhaps in my own particular premillennial-dispensational tradition, which constantly emphasized separation from the world, it was a bit more possible for me mistakenly to infer a certain emphasis on the transcendent. We were taught to "walk by the Spirit" and not "gratify the desires of the flesh" (Gal 5:16). So I memorized a great deal of Scripture in order to "let the word of Christ dwell in [me] richly" (Col 3:16). Where I misapplied these ideas, however, was essentially in thinking that my purpose was to live entirely, or as much as possible, in a kind of cerebral state of divine ecstasy, and to "pray without ceasing" (1 Thess 5:17, KJV). But even in a cloistered monastery, could I have joined one, I would have found that the physical world was still present in my own body and in all my surroundings.

I believe that I did come to regard the physical world as, de facto, of little or no spiritual importance. It was there only incidentally and was often even something of a nuisance, presenting many near occasions of sin or at least distracting from godly things. It would soon pass away. The moments when I was studying the Bible or sitting in a church service were great highs, but such sublime and emotional experiences cannot be sustained around the clock; so I found myself going back and forth between what I thought was "walking in the flesh" (not aware of God) and "walking by the spirit" (thinking about God). It felt at times like toggling a switch between the two. It felt like compartmentalization and sometimes even like living a double life. I am referring not only to guilt over sinful

activities but to feeling "unspiritual" if I was not consciously thinking about God at every moment. Catholics,
too, make a distinction between being in a state of grace
and being in a state of sin, but in Catholicism one can still
be in a state of grace and not necessarily be thinking about
God at every moment—for example, when one is at work
or in the middle of playing sports—for one knows interiorly, even then, that all these activities are consecrated to
Him. In the same way, you do not have to be thinking of
your spouse at every moment you are apart to have the
inner confidence that you are still married. Of course, you
do wear a wedding ring as an outward symbol or reminder
of it. But even then, it is not possible to be conscious at
every moment of the ring's presence, since your mind is
otherwise occupied with your activities.

By God's grace, a friend who was exploring Catholicism
gave me the book *Evangelical Is Not Enough* by Thomas
Howard, and I saw myself being described in those pages.[2]
Having been raised as a Catholic until around age thir-
teen, I did remember the physical components of Catholic worship, though I had never really understood the
reasons for them and thought they were silly. Finally, a
light bulb turned on: I understood that God's kingdom
includes both the spiritual and the physical and that Catholic worship reflects that continuity, providing places
where heaven and earth, so to speak, can meet. There
is no need to compartmentalize. The creation is good. It
may become disordered by man, but it is not there merely
as some kind of annoying obstacle course man must
endure to get to heaven. Our Church teaches that the
physical creation will even be fully redeemed and that our

---

[2] Thomas Howard, *Evangelical Is Not Enough* (San Francisco: Ignatius Press, 1984).

bodies will rise again, physically, so some dimension of physicality is here to stay.

In this life, the Real Presence of God in the physical Eucharist, the grace of the other physical sacraments, and the use of physical sacramentals and gestures imply a completely different mindset for living the Christian life around the clock, one that is holistic and does not compartmentalize body and soul or set them at odds. This is not to imply that Catholics never struggle with sin or concupiscence (as in Romans 7), but we have a clear context by which to understand this struggle and a clear sacramental remedy for it in Confession. We do not regard living bodily in the world as somehow unspiritual (or "in the flesh").

Mentally liberated, I began my own study of the Catholic faith, beginning with Catholic TV and the writings of Catholic convert Scott Hahn and other Catholic apologists, and a year later I went to Confession and came back into the Church. Some years later I became a certified catechist of the Catholic Church, and began to teach Confirmation classes and to speak to various Catholic groups and at Catholic universities and schools about a Catholic understanding of music and the Church's documents on music. This book is partly the outgrowth of those talks. I am happy to report that life in one unified compartment is great!

At some point it occurred to me that all I had learned about God and the Church should apply in some way to my own chosen profession of music, or rather that music must surely reflect these truths in some way. You may be wondering (as I was), "What really *is* music, in the most basic sense, that is, according to science? How do we perceive it, and why does it speak so meaningfully to our spirits? What is it about music that compels us to create and to hear it? What role should it play in my life?" For many years, my profession—composing mostly instrumental music for the classical concert hall—was yet another non-spiritual compartment to me, apart from God. I did pay lip service to the idea that I was composing music "for the glory of God", like Bach. But in practice, those words, "for the glory of God", were just too abstract to really apply to my work in any specific, musical way, other than as a matter of good intentions generally. So as a Catholic I began to explore music as a metaphor-in-sound for the link between immanence and transcendence—the same epiphany that brought me back to the Church—and then for other theological doctrines. I am hoping finally to share what I have learned with a broad Catholic readership, in language that does not require the reader to have any musical training whatsoever. There is a funny quote, source not entirely known, and existing in various permutations, that goes, "Trying to write about music is like trying to dance about architecture." I beg to differ with this, and will give it a try, in hopes of faithfully deepening both our understanding of our Church's teachings on music and our own aesthetic discernment, as regards the current musical culture, our Church's musical heritage, and the possible role that the Church could play in music in the future.

It is obvious that vocal music generally employs lyrics that communicate a message in words. In this book, I will be dealing not with lyrics (vocal texts) but with the tones of music, the pitches themselves, apart from words. So, unless otherwise stated, hereafter when I say "music", the reader should assume I am talking about instrumental music, without singers or words. But I will briefly note here that even songs with words do have a musical component that also communicates separately, usually in a way compatible with the words. We would immediately recognize an incompatibility or mixed message if we heard

the words to the song "Mary Had a Little Lamb" sung
to the music of the Beatles' "Helter Skelter", or if we
heard the words to the song "Get Happy" sung to the
minor-key funeral processional music from *The Godfather.*

With each of my music degrees, I either minored in or
otherwise studied art history. During my doctoral study
in music at the University of Michigan, I was fortunate
to complete a cognate with the very long-lived and
renowned German art theorist and perceptual psychol-
ogist Rudolf Arnheim (1904–2007). His magnum opus
was *Art and Visual Perception* (1954).[3] His groundbreaking
ideas were based largely upon applying Gestalt psychology
to the perception of visual art. Under his personal guidance, I attempted to apply his ideas about art to music.
Professor Arnheim also introduced me to the writings
of the famous American aesthetic philosopher Susanne
K. Langer (1895–1985), best known for her book about
the perception of music, *Philosophy in a New Key* (1942).[4]
Langer's work shed further light on some of the conclu-
sions about music I had been reaching in my study of
Arnheim's work.

However, to my knowledge, no one has yet attempted
to examine these fascinating concepts through the lens of
theology. So, in the spirit of Blessed John Henry Newman's *The Idea of a University,*[5] which calls theology the
ideal hub around which all inquiry should interconnect, I
will humbly attempt—though I am not a proper theolo-
gian myself—to at least start that discussion in my second

[3] Rudolf Arnheim, *Art and Visual Perception* (Berkeley, Calif.: University of
California Press, 1954).
[4] Susanne K. Langer, *Philosophy in a New Key*, 3rd ed. (Cambridge, Mass.:
Harvard University Press, 1957).
[5] John Henry Cardinal Newman, *The Idea of a University* (South Bend, Ind.:
University of Notre Dame Press, 1982).

chapter, but mainly in regard to my own area of music, with only a few brief mentions of visual art.

As this inquiry will deal further with the doctrines of immanence and transcendence, I need to further clarify the term *transcendence*, which has been used in general discourse with a variety of meanings and connotations. We have heard of Eastern transcendental meditation and the New England Transcendentalists. There is also the transcendentalism of Immanuel Kant, of German Idealism, and of German Romanticism, and the more mundane use of the term *transcendent* to say that something has broader implications than its immediate context. And there is, in popular usage, some vague and ill-defined, feel-groovy, mystical kind of transcendence, as in "That dinner was so delicious that it transported me to a place of sublime transcendence." Or it is equated with a vague "spirituality", as in "I'm spiritual but not religious." While some of these secular usages may be applied to music, I will keep my own use of *transcendence* as close as possible to the definition given in this introduction: the fact that God indwells every particle of the natural world but also exists independent of it, created it, and controls it. When you consider sound (including music) as physical molecules moving through the atmosphere—molecules too small to see but perceptible by the mechanisms of the human ear—then sound, music, and hearing also comprise physical matter indwelled yet transcended by God. If that previous sentence sounded curiously scientific, do not worry; it will be explained in chapter 2.

Likewise, let me expound upon and clarify *immanence* just a bit further. Someone may ask, "If God is already immanent in every atom and cell of my body, then how can the Holy Spirit 'indwell' me as a Christian? Isn't He there already?" The answer to that question in theology is fairly easy, if still a mystery. God is immanent in the *matter* of each person's physical body, whether that person is a Christian or not. But His Holy Spirit indwells our whole person, both spirit and body (*CCC* 364) in a special way, as His "temple" through Baptism (*CCC* 1265).[6] Our spiritual soul (see chapter 6 for a discussion of this term) animates our body in this life but is transcendent to it and will live on when our body and soul separate at death. On the Last Day, they will be reunited at the resurrection of the dead, as we affirm in the Nicene Creed at Mass.

This leads us on a brief side trip to consider the Eucharist, which, as the crucial "source and summit of the Christian life" (*CCC* 1324), is the principal lens through which we will regard music. When a friend says he cannot believe in the Real Presence of Christ in the Eucharist, I like to ask this question: "What happens when a human egg is fertilized and a woman becomes pregnant?" The answer, according to both Protestants and Catholics, is that a brand-new human soul is created by God. Then I ask, "If you can believe that a new, invisible soul is miraculously created within the matter of a tiny fertilized egg in a pregnant woman, why do you find it so difficult to believe that the invisible Spirit of Christ, likewise, can animate and transform the matter of the bread and wine? Both are supernatural events."

At conception, while the outward matter of the new child looks like nothing more than a lump of human cells, it is, in fact, a new individual human person. Moreover, as a member of the human family, this individual is endowed with a human soul, with the faculties of memory,

---

[6] Throughout this book, *CCC* will be used to refer to the *Catechism of the Catholic Church*, 2nd ed. (Vatican City: Libreria Editrice Vaticana / Washington, D.C.: United States Catholic Conference, 2000).

intelligence, and will. Since these faculties are spiritual and not strictly material, the Church affirms "that every spiritual soul is created immediately by God ... and also that it is immortal" (*CCC* 366). If you can believe in such a miraculous transformation of tiny reproductive germ cells into a new, immortal human person, then it should not be too hard to believe in the transformation of the Eucharistic matter into the person of Christ. This is the greatest gift He left with us, a gift by which we can experience His actual presence in the immanent, physical world.

That Christ is truly present in the Eucharist was the teaching of the Church at the time of the apostles and their earliest succeeding generations, according to first- and second-century historical records of worship. The Real Presence of Christ in the Eucharist was, for the early Church, a literal, face-value exegesis of the "Bread of Life" discourse in John 6 (Evangelicals consistently take Scripture at face value, but curiously, they make an exception for this passage.) When you consider that John's Gospel, dated by both Catholic and Protestant scholars at around A.D. 90, was written after, or around the same time as, several early nonscriptural but nonetheless legitimate historical Church records affirming that the Eucharist was considered to be not merely a remembrance but a sacrifice and the Real Presence of Christ, a literal interpretation of John 6 becomes all the more compelling. These documents include the *Didache*, a first-century manual of worship and catechesis; the writings of Clement of Rome, third successor to Saint Peter as bishop of Rome, dating to A.D. 80; the letters of Ignatius of Antioch, third bishop of Antioch, written A.D. 80–110; and a bit later, the testimonies of apologist Saint Justin Martyr, written A.D. 130–160, all of which confirm that the doctrine of the Real Presence was the normal belief about the Eucharist in the early Church.

was thinking
just thinking
of this today

So, just as God is both immanent and transcendent in the Eucharist, although in a very special way, and is also immanent and transcendent in a newly conceived human soul and person, *music is an ordinary substance (sound waves) imbued with an extraordinary ability to symbolize or mimic traits of human personhood.* Unlike the Eucharist or human conception, though, sound waves do not become a person— but they do appear to take on a "personality". This may make music seem an almost supernatural incarnation, but let us not become confused. Music does *not* involve a real miracle but is only a metaphor for a miracle, or a reflection of a miracle. As charmed and mesmerized and captivated as we may be by this "human" property of music, music itself is not to be an object of worship; this would be idolatry. Ultimately, we can appreciate and understand music properly and fully only as a symbol or reflection of the true "source and summit" miracle, the transubstantiation of bread and wine into the Eucharist. (We will return more fully to this in chapter 7.) Music must be neither an end in itself nor a way to bring glory to oneself. Properly ordered, music exists as a signpost on the road of life, with a big arrow pointing out the Way toward the Creator. If the natural creation represents an outpouring of God's love, atom for atom, molecule for molecule, cell for cell, then the invisible molecules of music can be heard by God's creatures as the glorious soundtrack to the great cornucopia of His love, an organic flowering of abundantly multiplying beauty. In chapter 2, we will explore the specific mechanics of how this musical symbolism works. But first we need to understand what music really is.

CHAPTER ONE

How Music Communicates as Physical Matter

Music's Invisibility

We all know by experience that music consists of sounds in the air that we can hear with the ear but not see with the naked eye. Music's invisibility has always seemed fundamentally mysterious and magical to me: ephemeral wisps of lovely sound that float by and tease us, then evaporate into nowhere as quickly as they came. It might even be tempting to conclude that music's invisibility is just like that of the angels. However, it is not quite so. The *Catechism of the Catholic Church* defines angels as creatures that are entirely "spiritual, non-corporeal" (*CCC* 328), that is, without any sort of body or physical matter. Music, on the other hand, is a natural, physical phenomenon, like the wind. Wind, too, is invisible, but we know that it is made of air in motion, and air is full of physical matter—the tiny molecules of numerous gases, including the oxygen we breathe. We can feel the wind and observe its effects on other physical matter, such as flags and leaves. Like the wind, which as our Lord explained to Nicodemus cannot be seen but rustles the trees (Jn 3:8), music can rustle (or rather, vibrate) our eardrums.

Even radio waves are physical. Although they are also invisible to the eye, they are no more magical or supernatural

Music is physical yet invisible

than regular sound waves. They cannot be seen or heard because they lie beyond the frequency spectrum of human perception, though they can be easily "heard" and played by radio sets. For similar reasons, dogs hear "silent" dog whistles for the simple reason that they perceive higher frequencies of vibration than humans. No animal, radio set, or device, however, can either see or hear angels naturally, since these are wholly supernatural and have no matter. Alas, the angels must remain elusive to us while we are on earth. But I will now demystify the invisible matter of sound and music and explain exactly how they work.

How Music Flows through the Air

If you ever dropped a pebble into a pond, you saw concentric rings, little circular waves, moving outward from where it landed (fig. 1). The force of the pebble hitting

Figure 1: Pond ripples.

the water caused the water around it to bunch up and peak a little higher than the surface of the water and move outward. This left a lack of water immediately behind the peak, like a little valley or trough, and then another peak of water rushed forward to fill the void, and so on, until all the energy was dissipated and the waves died out. You can observe much the same phenomenon in a stretching and compressing Slinky toy or even in highway traffic viewed from above.

The high points in the waves are called *compressions*, since they are more densely packed with water molecules, Slinky coils, or cars. The more loosely packed water valleys—or for Slinkys and traffic, the areas with wider gaps between objects, between the compressions—are called *rarefactions*. The substance through which the waves travel, be it water, metal, or air, is called the *medium*. Sound waves, including musical tones, are produced in the medium of the air when a physical source such as a vibrating piano string or the vibrating membrane of a loud speaker shoves the molecules of the air in front of it back and forth into compressions and rarefactions, like invisible pond waves. Imagine you are standing in a room near a speaker from which music is playing. If we could see the molecules of the atmospheric gases in this room magnified, they would look as shown in figure 2.

At this point it might be helpful to point out that while the earth's atmosphere comprises a mix of various gases (oxygen, hydrogen, carbon dioxide, etc.), there is no atmosphere at all in outer space but rather a vacuum, which means that there is no gaseous medium through which sound can travel. A vibrating string would make no audible sound in outer space! All those laser battles between spaceships in science-fiction movies would be completely silent, with neither the *shzoom!* sound effects

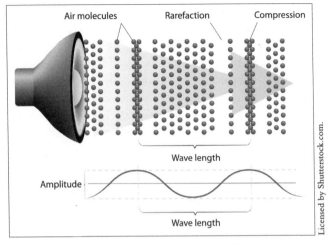

Figure 2: Sound wave molecules.

nor the exciting soundtrack. In college, I took a course on the physics of sound and was impressed one day when the professor brought in a doorbell ringing continuously inside a glass enclosure. He turned on a vacuum pump and began to suck the air out of the space, and the sound of the bell became softer and softer until it disappeared into silence in the total vacuum, even though you could still see the clapper hitting the bell vigorously inside. When he let the air back in, the sound became audible again.

A wave of sound or music flows through the medium of the air until it reaches your ear, specifically the membrane in the ear called the eardrum or tympanum. I will leave it to the reader to research how the ear works in greater detail, but suffice it to say here that the tympanum, a very thinly stretched membrane, responds to the sound waves with sympathetic vibrations, and then a system of fluids, tiny organs, and nerves behind it translates that into impulses sent to the brain, which perceives these as sound.

You can hear sympathetic vibrations on a piano by holding the pedal down on the piano and yelling into the piano strings; some of the strings will ring sympathetically.

The difference between a *note* and a *tone*, by the way, will become important as we go along, so here are some definitions. A *note* is a written symbol on a page. It is entirely visual; it has no sound. A *tone* is the sound made when someone actually plays or sings a note out loud. The specific type of written note dictates which pitch to play and how long to sustain it. (Of course, one can play a tone without needing to see a note first.) This is something like the distinction between a numeral (a written symbol on a page) and a number (an abstract concept). We might say that a note is in the realm of the transcendent, being abstract, symbolic, or conceptual, while a tone is in the realm of the immanent, being a concrete actualization of the note played out loud as a physical object of sound in the atmosphere, though consisting entirely of microscopic matter. We will discuss this more later.

Music as a Sculpture in Sound

We have dealt thus far with just one tone at a time, like a violin continuously playing a single, held tone, launching a steady stream of regular molecular compressions and rarefactions through the atmosphere. Now let us deal with more complex "sound sculptures in the air"—whole pieces of music, which take many tones as their material. It may be helpful to use visual analogies like sculpture to help us "see" music. If we could spray-paint the air where music is playing, making the particles visible, we would be able to see its various shapes, as in figure 2 above. We cannot, of course, simply paint the air, but if we could, it might be

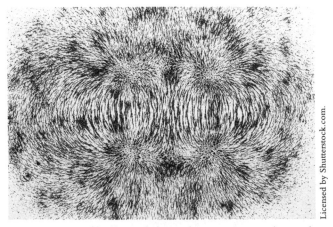

Licensed by Shutterstock.com.

Figure 3: Iron filings, with horseshoe magnet underneath.

something like putting iron filings on a sheet of paper with a magnet underneath. This causes shapes to form around the magnetic poles to reveal invisible "waves" of magnetism (fig. 3).

In fact, we can see something like this when sound transmitted through a microphone is represented electronically on an oscilloscope or, thanks to audio engineering software, on a computer screen (fig. 4). It may not look as beautiful as it sounds! I would not want to have this picture hanging on my wall, but I do nevertheless enjoy *hearing* figure 4 when it is manifested in sound as the first

Figure 4: A waveform graph of the first eight tones of Beethoven's Fifth Symphony.

five measures of Beethoven's Fifth Symphony. The complex, fuzzy shapes in figure 4 do not look like the simple waves illustrated in figure 2 because they do not illustrate a single sustained tone but rather a combination of many tones played by many different instruments, which interfere with each other in a variety of ways to form a complex waveform.

In summary, we have established as a foundation for our discussion that musical sound, invisible and seemingly ephemeral, is not a mysterious, unknowable, magical force but a real, physical object made up of particles of gaseous matter, too small to see with the naked eye, moving through the atmosphere. As such, it is made up of the materials of the natural creation, just as much as trees, flowers, soil, or rocks. We have established that God is immanent in all matter, including the physical molecules that make up sound. He is also in all the pigments and components of oil paint. But just as paint is not the same thing as a painting, neither is sound the same thing as a piece of music. Both consist of natural elements that humans use as raw materials to craft a painting or a piece of music. Thus, it has been said that artists do not really "create" anything but only reorganize the materials God has created. Nonetheless, it seems fair to say that they do employ "creativity" in doing so. We will come back to that later.

It might be good to remark here that if God is indeed immanent in the raw materials artists use, which are His own wholly good creation, how terrible a thing it is for us to "reorganize" them into obscene or blasphemous art or music! How would you feel if you had spent many loving hours of needlework, pouring your whole self into the sewing of a beautiful handbag for your dearest friend, and then this friend used it in turn only to carry rotten garbage

to the bin? God has lovingly given us very beautiful materials and is in them and sustains their existence at every
moment, and so we have a responsibility to use them to
make the finest art of which we are capable, with right
intentions. The same goes for how we treat those invisible
gaseous atoms of music flowing in waves through the air.
I sometimes wonder, if only we could see God's immanence glowing in everything He has created, including
all of nature, even down to the atoms that make up each
thing, what a wondrously sacred world we might perceive
and inhabit.

CHAPTER TWO

How Music Communicates in the Psychology of Perception

Music as Shapes in Motion

Now let us explore how these sculptures in sound affect us interiorly, move us, agitate, scare, or seem to caress us tenderly. Have you ever had a chill up your spine when hearing a thrilling piece of music? Or wiped away a few tears after hearing an achingly beautiful melody? By contrast, how often have you had a chill up your spine or teared up upon seeing a sculpture in stone? The latter is certainly possible, especially to the truly sensitive art lover, but I would speculate that for most of us these visceral reactions happen more often in response to music. There is a reason for this: music, like sculpture, does also consist of "shapes", but in the case of music, these shapes are *in motion* as waves in the air, as we saw in the previous chapter.

The American philosopher Susanne K. Langer called such shapes in motion *dynamic forms*.[1] She cites a waterfall as an example of a dynamic form that you can see.[2] A waterfall has a definite shape, be it like a round column or a sheet (depending on its width) in the air (fig. 5). The shape

---

[1] Susanne K. Langer, *Feeling and Form: A Theory of Art* (Charles Scribner & Sons, 1953), 125, 312.
[2] Susanne K. Langer, *Problems of Art* (Charles Scribner & Sons, 1957), 48.

Licensed by Shutterstock.com.

Figure 5: Waterfall as a dynamic form.

itself is static—it holds its form and does not significantly change—and yet from moment to moment it is made up of entirely different molecules of water. We might even go so far as to say that a waterfall is a shape created by motion itself! If you cut off the source of water upstream and took away its motion, the shape would cease to exist.

How exactly is music like a waterfall? The essential matter of music is particles streaming through the air, like droplets of water might stream down from a high cliff. So had you been watching the computer screen depicted in figure 4 as the music was being registered, you would have seen the screen gradually fill in from left to right. If you wanted to imagine this as a "waterfall of tones", you could simply turn your computer screen 90 degrees, to the vertical, and see it fill in from top to bottom (fig. 6).

A single, held tone is a clearer analog to the waterfall, as its shape will remain uniform, very generally speaking. But the waterfall-in-sound of a complex musical composition does not yield a steady, straight column. It is always changing shape, just as the waveform in figure 6 varies continually in shape. Nonetheless, at every given moment the music does have a definite, clear shape. To illustrate this with a slow-motion example, the "blobs" in a lava lamp are always morphing and shifting, but if you were to take a photo of the lamp at any point in time, you would see what specific shape the blobs had at that precise moment. So it is with the particles caught up in complex sound waves. For the next part of our discussion, let us call these shapes in the air "the forms of music".

How We Relate to the Forms of Music

Langer postulated that human beings experience an infinite variety of bodily and mental sensations that she called the *forms of feeling*.[3] By *feeling*, she means "all that can be felt", not merely emotions. Feelings might include mental or muscular tensions, for example, or various kinds of relaxation. They may manifest themselves or be interpreted

Figure 6: Digital waveform graph, vertical.

[3] Langer, *Feeling and Form*, 397.

"can feel w/o emotion"

by our conscious mind as emotions, but they may also affect us in subtler ways. For example, one can get a certain feeling by splashing cold water on one's own face yet not have any particular emotion about it. We may jump at a surprise, feel the wind on our cheeks, have a satisfying sneeze, feel a baby's soft skin, or experience such "feelings" in a thousand other ways. Whereas we have a finite number of English words to express various emotions—as large as that number might be—the forms of feeling are theoretically infinite in variety and could never be all named and catalogued using language. Because such feelings take place and develop through time (even if briefly), they can, like music, take a shape or a form over the course of their duration. And because these forms of feeling are in motion, changing and developing through time, they can also be called dynamic forms. If you could graph them, they might swell in the middle and shrink as they go away, or else have some other such contours. They would surely also look just as complex as figure 4, considering the many nerve endings and mental impressions that are in play. One of the greatest wonders in all creation is, of course, the human creature, body, brain, and mind, with millions of impulses happening in the brain, and an army of nerve endings shooting out messages in the body that can be interpreted by the mind.

Langer proposes an isomorphism (in Greek, *iso* + *morphe* = "same shape") in the human mind whereby we can innately recognize forms of music as somehow congruent with some form of feeling we have experienced in the past. Music can conjure up in us the recollection of those particular feelings or even induce in us a kind of vicarious or sympathetic reaction to them.[4] A very obvious

relate music to our emotion

Theory

---

[4]Langer, *Philosophy in a New Key*, 238.

example of this is the sound of teeth chattering from the cold, as depicted by the "chattering" violins in Vivaldi's "Winter" concerto from *The Four Seasons*; he even explicitly labels them as such in the score. Similarly, the sounds of weeping may be easily imagined in the first string theme of Tchaikovsky's Fourth Symphony, and the sounds of human sighs in the opening of Brahms' Fourth Symphony. This is where a leap of imagination may be necessary, as we have no technically reliable way to map visually the human forms of feeling. There are various kinds of brain scans, but none of them graphically represent any specific form of feeling. So there is, to my knowledge, so far no physiological or scientific way to prove Langer's 1942 theory, and her work has gone in and out of fashion, though it still seems plausible to many.

It sounds plausible because we can all broadly, if not scientifically, agree from our collective experience that a generally agitated-sounding piece of music tends to invite a good number of us to respond in some kind of nervous way, while a soothing-sounding piece of music tends to relax people. It has been so since the time that David played his harp for disturbed King Saul. But unlike spoken language, which has a finite number of synonyms for the adjectives *agitated* and *soothing*, music has a vast, if not infinite, number of "musical synonyms" that can represent countless shades of agitation or of tranquility, for which words are inadequate. Our nonlinguistic sensibilities seem to perceive, recognize, and respond to these multifarious states or forms in music, because in some way they share a congruent "shape".

But the question may be asked, So what? Why do we *care* so much about the fact that we recognize in music something congruous to our unspoken feelings? Could this recognition alone really be the reason we love certain pieces of music so passionately? Not entirely. Langer says that our own need for outward expression causes us to identify these symbols, latch on to them, and *objectify* them (i.e., recognize them as objects). "Art is the objectification of feeling", she writes.[5] That is to say, we identify that the work of art is somehow speaking on our behalf, expressing in a "language" too deep for words what we wish we could find words to say. We find this very gratifying, vicariously, just as we do when a great orator says something we ourselves believe and long to utter, only so much more powerfully than we ever could have said it.

Music and the Interior Life

My work as a professional composer of instrumental music has also led me to dabble in writing words, not only prose (as in this book) but poetry and song lyrics. I can honestly attest that while instrumental music does have so many more "synonyms" for every "adjective", so many more nuanced "shades of melancholy", than language, sometimes music feels inadequate too. I could not, for example, have written this book as a piece of music and communicated through music what this book can communicate in words. I cannot compose a phrase for the oboe that makes everyone think suddenly of a horse or an ice cream cone or a tree. *That is because the forms of music and the forms of feeling remain in the realm of the symbolic or abstract, what we Catholics call the "interior life".* In Romans 8:26, Saint Paul might be referring to this kind of interior communication when he says that the

---

[5] Susanne K. Langer, *Mind: An Essay on Human Feeling*, abridged ed. (Baltimore: Johns Hopkins Press, 1999).

Holy Spirit prays for us in groanings too deep for words, when we cannot express to God in mere words what we want to say in prayer. While in this verse the groans are God's, we vicariously identify with them and interiorly participate in them. Man's longings reach far beyond his capacity to verbalize them. I do not mean to imply that Saint Paul requires music to be playing during prayer. I mean only that these silent groanings are of an interior nature; some people may feel that they experience them silently in the presence of the Blessed Sacrament at Adoration. I have personally, though rarely, had the experience of feeling myself praying to God in a wordless and silent way while composing instrumental music, as if carried to heaven on the wings of the musical shapes my imagination was conceiving, before writing them down. It may be possible to pray through music as an instrumentalist too. If it is true, as Saint Augustine says, that "he who sings, prays twice" (once through lyrics and once through music), then one might logically conclude, "He who plays the violin prays once." I do not know; we are in the realm of mystery.

Although Langer's theory may be impossible to prove, it cannot be disproved either. I believe that it is entirely plausible in some respects. I will unscientifically but nonetheless boldly assert: Our collective experience bears out that there must be *some* kind of human sensory and perceptive mechanism relating the forms of music to familiar bodily feelings and mental states beyond the reach of language, by means of which music can trigger human feelings (in the broadest sense) as a response, provided the listener is acculturated to the musical style, is listening attentively, and is disposed to perceive them. (These are three crucial qualifications, by the way.) The Mayo Clinic reports remarkable responses to music by otherwise unresponsive Alzheimer's patients.[6] Of course, Langer's writings present many other concepts as well, most in the realm of the discipline of philosophy, and I have taken the liberty of simplifying her sometimes difficult writing while trying to stay true to its essential meaning.

How Our Experience of Natural Forces Influences the Way We Hear Music

Rudolf Arnheim's theories are complementary to Langer's but much less arcane and abstract. He names several specific kinds of forms in visual art that can relate to specific, identifiable bodily and mental states, and for which we might propose at least some musical counterparts. We will survey a handful of them. These also have to do with shapes, and even with dynamic shapes. Arnheim says, "Visual *experience* is dynamic"—that is, even perfectly still paintings and sculptures are *perceived* as implying potential motion, through "an interplay of directed tensions".[7] Let me illustrate this with a simple example. If you are like me, when you see a picture frame hanging a bit crooked on your wall, you feel tension and an urge to get up and straighten it. This can be awkward if you are visiting someone's home and see it on *their* wall, or if a visitor goes around straightening pictures on *your* walls. Some of us just cannot help ourselves! Why?

Arnheim goes into some depth about how artists exploit the human need for equilibrium. The second law

---

[6]Jonathan Graff-Redford, "Can music help someone with Alzheimer's?", Mayo Clinic, last updated April 20, 2019, https://www.mayoclinic.org /diseases-conditions/alzheimers-disease/expert-answers/music-and-alzheimers /faq-20058173.

[7]*Art and Visual Perception*, 11.

of thermodynamics describes how energy must dissipate toward what is called *entropy* and reach a steady state of equilibrium. For example, if you shake a glass of water and set it down, the water on the surface will tumble around and then gradually settle down until it is flat and still and level. The molecules in the water will seek symmetry and balance until they achieve it. If we leave a glass of cold water in a warm room, over time the thermal energy in the warm air will disperse into the water, and the two will equalize in temperature. When we are on a small boat in rough seas, our bodies lean to and fro precariously, with the scary possibility of falling overboard; we give thanks when at last we set foot on solid ground. Experiencing such discomfort in many ways in our lives (hiking on a steep hillside, riding on a carnival ride, etc.) fosters a natural aversion to imbalance and asymmetry in favor of safety, stability, and survival. So if that crooked picture frame on the wall is not in balance, it must be set straight. If it is leaning to the left, then the "directed tension" mentioned above requires we pull it back to the right, so that all will once more be right with the world.

Artists can create a subconscious feeling of directed tension in a painting by having people or objects (like tables) leaning off balance, in defiance of gravity, or even by having all the people in the painting looking in a certain direction, drawing our eyes over to see what they are all looking at. In music, composers can create a sense of tension and imbalance by using dissonances (combinations of tones that sound discordant, due to their complex frequency ratios) that sound as if they need to resolve into the relaxed equilibrium of consonance (harmonious combinations of tones in simpler frequency ratios that feel "at rest" together). Or they can create a sense of tension by means of irregular or unbalanced phrasing and rhythms. In the case of rhythmic tension, such as irregular and unpredictable syncopations (afterbeats), we have a desire for a regular and predictable beat to return, as someone with a heart murmur longs for his irregular heartbeat to return to normal.

Arnheim also cites *anisotropic space* as a corollary to our desire for left-right balance, because it has to do with vertical space. *Anisotropic* comes from the Greek *anisos* ("not the same") and *tropos* ("turn")—that is, when you turn from the horizontal to the vertical. We live with the force of gravity and take it for granted, but in fact it is always pulling us down, and we are often working against it, even, for example, just standing up. "To rise upward is to overcome resistance", he claims. "It is always a victory. To descend or fall is to surrender to the pull from below."[8] Thus, in art, the mats we put between the glass and the pictures when framing them often have a wider vertical space on the bottom, which somehow feels balanced, as if to push the picture up to compensate for gravity. The composition of many paintings reflects this same sensibility. Narrowing shapes, like church steeples, can thrust our vision upward to heaven, from the wide to the narrow, just as the converging perspective lines in a painting can pull our eyes to the distance of farther, smaller objects.

In music, we have the overtone series (figure 7), which is naturally occurring. When you vibrate any string on a stringed instrument (e.g., violin, harp, guitar, piano), that string's main pitch and volume come from the oscillation of its entire length, back and forth. However, smaller segments of that string (halves, thirds, fourths, etc.) are also simultaneously vibrating, producing a series of other pitches, higher and higher the shorter the segments become. We do not notice these additional tones in their

---

[8] Ibid., 30.

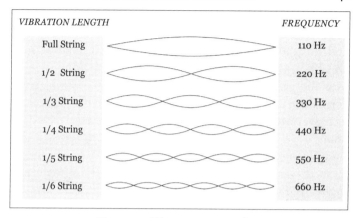

Figure 7: The overtone series.

own right because they are so much quieter than the main
tone of the full string and are therefore subsumed into it.
Nevertheless, they serve to color the tone of the string; this
"tone color" is called *timbre*. It so happens that the spacing
of these tones, when written on a musical staff, is widest
between the lowest tones and then gradually narrows as
the series gets higher. When looking at the printed music
for a chorale, such as a church hymn, anyone (without
reading music) can see that the vertical distance between
the lower notes in the chords is most often wider than that
between the higher notes. The overtone series may illustrate something analogous to anisotropic space in sound,
with the foundation of gravity, as it were, represented by
the widest space—the octave, at the bottom of the series—
followed by a decreasing distance between tones as you go
up, like the narrowing church steeples mentioned above.

Pitch may be represented mathematically by looking at
the frequencies of tones. The frequency increases as the
pitch rises. For example, a string playing the A above middle C (the A to which orchestras tune before a concert)

vibrates at 440 hertz (or Hz, vibrations per second), while the A one octave above it vibrates twice as fast at 880 Hz, and the next A twice that at 1,760 Hz. When we hear an old-fashioned siren or a small engine revving up, we hear the pitch go up as the mechanism starts to spin faster and faster, and we sense with excitement the increasing energy. And as we hear a Dixieland clarinetist playing a rising scale—starting from the bottom of the instrument then lifting up to a note higher even than we imagined a clarinetist could play—that trajectory can give us the exciting feeling of taking off, flying, and escaping from gravity. Similarly, as the architect uses the anisotropic church-steeple effect mentioned above, he symbolically creates a sense of dynamic motion, thrusting our focus higher and higher toward the heavens. I have often noticed that clarinetists tend to lift up their shoulders as they go up a scale and then slump them down when descending. There is no technical reason for doing this.

Like Langer, Arnheim cites the Gestalt principle of isomorphism ("same shape") to describe how humans mentally organize and process a very complex world. Arnheim defines isomorphism as "the structural kinship between the stimulus pattern and the expression it conveys".[9] This reminds us of the correspondence Langer makes between the patterns or forms of music and the forms of feeling. However, Arnheim stresses this concept in broader terms, tying it to our tendency to relate shapes as much as possible to things that we know. This can involve *simplification*.[10] For example, we recognize and accept a child's crude drawing of a stick man or an elephant as a man or an elephant, even though it may look very little like the

[9] Ibid., 450.
[10] Ibid., 63.

real thing, because we associate it with the nearest familiar shape. We recognize a drawing of a cloud-shaped blob on top of a pillar as an image of a tree, even though trees come in thousands of shapes. If we had to memorize all of the thousands of forms a tree can take, we would either suffer from information overload or go mad. Thus, we group similar things into general categories that we can manage, such as "tree".

When listening to music, we tend likewise to "correct" or "forgive" mistakes. If a beginner band is supposed to play a chord perfectly together on a downbeat but instead hits it, *ker-flunk*, in a ragged manner, we still try to hear it as a clean attack. If a pop singer hits a tone a little flat, but close enough to the right pitch to make it clear what it was supposed to be, we try to give the benefit of the doubt and hear it as it was intended. → *when someone trips up*

Another way we use simplification to perceive the world is in dividing large sets of objects into smaller, bite-size portions that we can take in more easily. For instance, I have often been grateful that the numbers on my debit card are separated into groups of four rather than displayed as one long string of sixteen numbers. It makes them so much easier to read out loud to someone over the phone.

We also make sense of things through *grouping by similarity*.[11] For example, if we see a canvas full of red circles and green squares, we immediately and instinctively sort them into two groups. In a subtler way, an artist may use this property to relate two characters in a painting. For example, imagine a painting of a group of people, two of whom are wearing red cloaks—the only red in the whole painting. Even though they are on opposite sides of the painting—perhaps Romeo and Juliet at the Capulets'

[handwritten margin note: does this depend on / this person / necessarily / go that way / but it does / use... / will that situation / I think it's an example of it]

[11] Ibid., 80.

party just before they meet—we connect them together by color, and feel as though we have been secretly told that they will soon be together.

There are many musical counterparts to these concepts. Just like the numbers on a credit card, music is often parsed into bursts of a handful of melodic notes or individual chords at a time, clearly separate from each other. They form recognizable and often memorable units, as when you go away humming some tune you heard in the music. Sometimes a distinct musical idea appears in one key ("home", let's call it), and then in another higher key ("going away from home"), and then back in the first key ("returning home"), so that—like with the red cloaks in the above example—you can hear the contrast between tonal departure and return to the original key.

The point is that we normally "eat a meal" of music in small-enough "bites" for our minds to process and sort out, relating similar ideas, as when a theme recurs later in the music. However, in the case of much Modernist, atonal music, these recognizable units are not always present in small-enough or simple-enough bites to remember. We cannot process the very complex way the music is presented, as would be the case if the numbers on the credit card were all run together instead of in groups of four. If we cannot remember the musical units, then we cannot recognize when they return, or group them by similarity, as described above, and so the typical way of perceiving music breaks down. We will further discuss atonal music in chapter 4, but my point here is that not only the dissonance (discordance) and lack of a tune put people off from atonal music (these are often cited as the reasons for disliking it). The dislike can be just as much due to the sheer information overload or the lack of the simplification into perceptible bites. This music usually does contain certain resonances and similarities, but they are too complex for most people to remember and relate to one another aurally, so only a few elite listeners can even comprehend, much less enjoy, it. Advanced music students can be taught to find and mark the similarities on paper in the score, but hearing these without the aid of seeing them highlighted on the score is far more difficult. The music will sound random to most ears. Incidentally, my observation is that some students, having been taught to understand such music, feel they have been admitted to an elite, secret society and, thus honored, help to perpetuate it through the next generation of students.

How Spoken Language Influences the Way We Hear Music

Let us move on to a comparison between music and spoken language that might also account for our ability to relate to music in a familiar way. Music may be said to be heard through time in units comparable to words (*notes*), sentences (several notes in a musical *phrase*), and paragraphs (a *period*, or group of phrases). In the case of the last two, the phrases are often separated by a short pause called a *rhythmic caesura*. Music may be said to have grammar and syntax, with its system of scales and harmonic progressions. It may rise and fall in pitch contour like our speaking voices do, rising, for example, at the end of a phrase to give the impression of a question. It may mimic the kinds of rhythms and volume levels our speaking voices use when yelling angrily or when soothing an infant to sleep. Anyone who has seen the *Peanuts* TV cartoons, where the schoolteacher's voice is mimicked by the *wa-wa* of a muted trombone, can understand these comparisons.

The relationship between spoken language and music has been written about extensively, so rather than trying to cover it all here, I will leave it to the reader to explore some of these sources on his own.[12] I will share here some of my own original research from a more clearly Catholic perspective, which I have lectured about at Catholic colleges under the title "Discovering Prayer and Music through the Figures of Rhetoric". I will explain how some of the formulas of language usage described in the classical discipline of rhetoric have counterparts in Catholic liturgy and in music. (I will not be breaking my earlier promise to avoid the subject of song lyrics here, because I will be talking mainly about the musical rhythms and patterns accompanying sung words rather than about those words.)

Rhetoric seems a daunting word, but it refers simply to the art of putting words together to make a persuasive argument. It can also refer to a catalogue of ways to turn a catchy phrase, so as to communicate effectively. As a discipline, and as a subject that students study in school, it can be traced back to 2000 B.C. Skipping ahead in time, we can note that Aristotle wrote a book called *The Art of Rhetoric* (late fourth century B.C.), which Saint Augustine (b. A.D. 354) brought into the Christian tradition. It was taught in the very first universities and in Western education up until the end of the nineteenth century. Nowadays it is rightly being revived as a curriculum subject among Catholics and Protestants in the current classical education movement.

Historically, those who taught rhetoric understood that language has a tendency to degenerate or get "dumbed down" if not carefully preserved by means of study. We

---

[12] One source that is enjoyable and understandable to anyone is "The Unanswered Question", a series of Norton Lectures given by Leonard Bernstein at Harvard in 1973, which were televised on network TV and are now freely available on the Internet with a simple search.

can see this illustrated in today's tendency to say that pretty much everything one likes is "amazing", in lieu of any of a hundred other more apt adjectives. Having your child study rhetoric can help him become a potentially eloquent spokesperson for just about anything. The liturgy of our Mass, with its beautiful and eloquent language, exalts our worship with the excellence of its rhetoric, and we are ennobled by it as Catholics.

I will mention here in passing what the classical Romans called the five *canons* (or rules) of rhetoric and give a musical counterpart to each.

1. The first canon is *inventio*, meaning inventiveness or imagination, what we would call creativity. Composers especially require this trait in making their "musical arguments", as do performers who either improvise (as in jazz) or somehow bring a personal interpretation to the score.

2. The second canon is *dispositio*, meaning how the argument is organized, perhaps in some logical progression that the hearer can follow point by point. In music, this could be compared to the overall form of a piece of music. In response to this need for organization, several standard classical forms of music were developed that many composers have employed, such as the sonata–allegro form or rondo form.

3. The third canon is *elocutio*, meaning the tailoring of the style to the culture of the specific audience being addressed. In music, this might be compared with genre. You might make your most effective case via a string quartet with one audience, and via a country-western song with another audience. In film music, you would adapt the style of the music to what is happening on the screen.

4. The fourth canon is *memoria*, meaning the ability to speak extemporaneously from memory rather than to have to read one's speech. In music, this could take the form of an improvisation without the need to follow a score, or simply of memorizing one's music for a concert, which is more impressive to the audience. Obviously, in vocal forms of music like opera and musical theater, carrying a score around the stage would distract the audience and break the spell of the drama. Many who have seen Archbishop Fulton Sheen's *Life Is Worth Living* telecasts have been deeply impressed by the power of *memoria* on the part of the host, who did his eloquent presentations live and completely from memory, without cue cards.

5. The fifth canon is *pronuntiatio*, meaning the speaker's delivery, including volume, pitch, pace of speaking, posture, gestures, and facial expressions. (Sheen again comes to mind.) In music, these things all have a great deal to do with an effective performance. For example, music students learning to play an instrument tend to play everything at about the same volume and have to be taught to emphasize the contrast between soft and loud passages, for greater expression and emotion.

These are the five canons of rhetoric. Now, the *figures* of rhetoric, mentioned above, are specific formulas (I know of around 450 that have been catalogued) for saying something with a bit more flare and crispness or for emphasizing its meaning in a certain way. By surveying just a handful of them, we can get a sense of how they work and make the point I wish to make here about music (Table 1).

The survey could go on and on. For example, there are many musical examples of the figure of rhetoric called

Table 1

Rhetorical Figure	Definition	Examples
Epizeuxis (or *geminatio*, iteration)	Repetition of words consecutively for emphasis	LITERATURE • "*A horse, a horse*, my kingdom for a horse!" (Shakespeare, *Richard III*) LITURGY/SCRIPTURE • "*Holy, Holy, Holy* Lord God of hosts" (*Roman Missal*) • "*My God, my God*, why have you forsaken me?" (Ps 22:1; Mt 27:46) MUSIC • Beethoven, Symphony no. 5, beginning • "*Hallelujah! Hallelujah!*" ("Hallelujah Chorus", in Handel, *Messiah*) • "*Jingle bells, jingle bells*, jingle all the way" ("Jingle Bells")
Tricolon	Three parallel elements of approximately the same length occurring together in a series	LITERATURE • "*Veni, vidi, vici*" (Shakespeare, *Julius Caesar*) LITURGY/SCRIPTURE • "Through *my fault*, through *my fault*, through *my most grievous fault*" (*Roman Missal*) MUSIC • Mozart, Symphony no. 40, opening
Antithesis	Juxtaposition of parallel opposites for contrast	LITERATURE • "*To be* or *not to be*" (Shakespeare, *Hamlet*) LITURGY/SCRIPTURE • "You have heard that it was said, '. . . *hate your enemy*.' But I say to you, *Love your enemies*." (Mt 5:43–44)

(*continued*)

Table 1 (*continued*)

Rhetorical Figure	Definition	Examples
Antithesis (*continued*)		MUSIC • Mozart, *Eine kleine Nachtmusik*, first two phrases (one ascends, the other descends)
Chiasmus (or antimetabole)	Repetition of ideas or words in inverted order	LITERATURE • "Ask not what *your country can do for you*; ask what *you can do for your country*." (U.S. President John F. Kennedy, inaugural address, 1961) ORATION • "This is not the end. It is not even *the beginning of the end*. But it is, perhaps, *the end of the beginning*." (Winston Churchill, 1942) LITURGY/SCRIPTURE • "Forgive us our trespasses as we forgive those who trespass against us." (Mt 6:12) MUSIC • George Gershwin, "I Got Rhythm", first two phrases (C–D–F–G, G–F–D–C)
Epistrophe	Ending every line, phrase, or paragraph with same line	LITERATURE • "Will you eat them in a house? / I do not like green eggs and ham, I do not like them, Sam I am. / Will you eat them with a mouse? / I do not like green eggs and ham, I do not like them, Sam I am." (Dr. Seuss, *Green Eggs and Ham*)

(*continued*)

Table 1 (*continued*)

Rhetorical Figure	Definition	Examples
Epistrophe (*continued*)		LITURGY/SCRIPTURE • Responsorial Psalm in the Mass • Litany of the Saints ("Saint N., pray for us.") MUSIC • "I Remember It Well" (Frederick Loewe, *Gigi*)

onomatopoeia. This term refers to any word that imitates the sound of the thing it describes, like *pow* or *meow*. The closest musical representation of human weeping I know may be found in the first theme (played by the strings after an introduction of about a minute and a half) of Tchaikovsky's Symphony no. 4, first movement, mentioned above. It uses a repeated descending melody that closely mimics the descending pitch of sobs in human crying, and it grows more and more anxious or weepy as the movement goes on. The first theme of Brahms' Symphony no. 4, first movement—played, again, by the strings, at the very beginning—closely mimics a series of melancholy human sighs in a series of two-note patterns. Is it any wonder that these pieces call forth in us a sympathetic response? And so, spoken language, with its persuasive pitch inflections and its rhetorical patterns and arguments, gives us a clue as to why we respond to some music as if it were already an old friend, somehow familiar.

In summary, we have explored some possible psychological and physiological explanations for why we relate and respond to music. Music seems very strongly to present us with aural analogs or sonic symbols for the "shapes" and states of being that are already familiar to us from our own catalogue of bodily and mental-psychic states, or else with analogs to human speech patterns. We tend to *objectify*—that is, recognize as objects—these physical (though invisible) shapes in the air and vicariously identify with them. We allow them to express back to us, or on our behalf, what we ourselves have felt as humans, echoing and affirming our own experience.

CHAPTER THREE

How Music Communicates
to the Emotions

So far we have seen that a piece of music may offer up
aural cues as a kind of call that can elicit a felt response
in listeners, and that response can be described in terms
of feelings or emotions. Those cues or triggers, although
uniquely interpreted by each individual listener, are more
or less fixed in the structure of the music itself, so that
every time that piece of music is accurately performed,
those same cues can be perceived. For example, multi-
tudes of people have independently confirmed over many
years that Samuel Barber's *Adagio for Strings* (1936, known
to some from its use in the soundtrack to the 1986 movie
Platoon) has a set of innate properties that can trigger some
general form (if not exactly the same form) of sadness or
melancholy in most listeners. The music, for its part, is
thus "doing its job", just as a priest may be doing his
job in giving a great homily. Yet, just as some parishioners may be distracted or sleeping during the homily,
even though it is powerful, not every listener will actively
respond the dynamic forms of music. It takes two to
tango, as they say—in our case, the music and the listener.
Since our emotional response to music depends so much
on how we listen, I want to lay a little groundwork on the

listening experience before getting into the main topic of this chapter.

Ways We Listen to Music

Perhaps you have had the experience of being deeply moved by a piece of music on one occasion and then not feeling much emotion when hearing the very same piece of music on another occasion. There is no guarantee that a piece of music will elicit the same spontaneous reaction. Two people sitting next to each other at a concert may both experience much the same emotion when hearing a piece of music, or one person may experience emotion while the person next to him does not. Clearly, the listener's own subjective disposition, as we Catholics would call it, is crucial to his response to music. Much depends upon the mental and emotional state of the listener just prior to hearing the music, the presence or absence of mental distractions, and the manner of listening. Let me address what I mean by "manner of listening" before we go on.

Some people tend to listen to music in terms of other things with which they associate it. For example, someone might be preoccupied with the fact that a certain song had been "our song" while they were dating their spouse, calling to mind the first romantic moment when they bonded by listening to it together. Or the piece may be a composition in which they played the flute in the high school band, conjuring up memories of the band room. The marching band may have been playing a certain piece when you scored the winning touchdown in the big game, and so you will forever retain that association. Or the piece may have been first heard in a film: to return to the above example, some people have a hard time separating Barber's

Adagio from images of *Platoon*. In past generations, almost no one could hear Gioachino Rossini's overture to *William Tell* without thinking of the TV series *The Lone Ranger*.

Another type of listener may know something about music and be listening to it more analytically. This could take the form of noticing every detail of the performer's work, whether positively or critically: "He was flat on that note!" "Her tone sounds just like (insert name here)'s tone." It could take the form of analyzing the work itself: "Now we are beginning the development section." "That's a whole-tone scale!" "He stole that from Debussy!" Most college music majors go into this mode of listening at a certain point, because it is part of learning their craft, but when I hear it happening, I warn them that they may be listening so hard they miss the music, and that they may lose the innocent love of music that made them choose to major in music in the first place.

At the other extreme, some listeners do not pay attention to the particulars of the music at all but prefer to let the music wash over them like the ocean's tide and bathe in a sensual wash of gorgeous sound. For them, it is all about ambience and daydreaming of other things.

And then there are multitasking listeners, for whom all music is simply a background for doing other things. If they are at home, they put on music while washing dishes, talking on the phone, chatting at a dinner party, or simply playing solitaire on their computer. They cannot bear just to sit and give their whole attention to the music. There is nothing wrong with using music this way; I sometimes do it myself. But there are at least some occasions when I forbid myself from doing anything but listening attentively and exclusively to the music. It seems to me that multitasking in today's busy, sound-bite world, aided by today's technology, can present a detriment to any kind of deep experience, such as reading a great novel or praying deeply, and may wind up transforming us collectively into a more superficial culture, if it has not already.

Perhaps the ideal way of listening may be described as a combination of the best traits of all those listed above. The ideal listeners give the music its due attention and follow the narrative in it but without allowing critical analysis to interfere. They may have extramusical associations but do not allow those to distract from the music. They enjoy the sheer sound of the music but not at the expense of paying attention to what is going on in it. This is the kind of listener who I think has the best experience with music, and this type of listening is actually a skill that can be improved with a little conscious effort, by making time for it.

In addition to these basic ways of listening, I will mention a few more cultural types of listeners. There are passive and active listeners, meaning that some people passively accept whatever music is chosen for them by others, usually radio DJs, while others actively seek out and choose what to listen to, creating their own, often more diverse, playlists. There are also those I call "brand" listeners. These are people who listen to certain music because it is associated with the brand or personal style they wish to adopt. Maybe they are part of a motorcycle culture, a hipster culture, a classic rocker culture, a square dance and barbecue culture, a smooth-jazzy "wine and cheese" or artsy culture, and so on. Brand listeners seek to wear the right clothing, drive the right vehicle, wear the right hairstyle and jewelry, and listen to the right music to fit in and to advance or reinforce the image of themselves they wish to cultivate. Then there are dance- or rhythm-oriented listeners who seek out music like rap or hip-hop, with a primary emphasis on a danceable beat, whether or not they actually dance along with it. The angry listener, for his part, seeks out performers who never smile and who look angry in their photos, never use humor in their lyrics, and tend perhaps toward the sound of rage. This list could go on. All of these examples raise the question of *why* people choose the music they are listening to. I would like to propose that faithful Catholics be "active" and carefully select their own choice of music based upon the innate qualities of the music itself rather than upon some of the above criteria. Even music commercially marketed to Christians may exhibit musical mediocrity, so simply "branding" oneself by listening to "Christian music" is not necessarily the right approach. Ask yourself instead: Does the music (and not only the lyrics) exhibit some aspect of virtue, edification, beauty, truth, excellence, or goodness? We will return to this topic in chapters 4, 5, and 6.

Music as a Language of Expectation and Fulfillment

Leonard Meyer (1918–2007) advanced a theory about why music triggers our emotions, in his book *Emotion and Meaning in Music* (1956).[1] Meyer, like Langer and Arnheim, was influenced by Gestalt psychology and by other theorists of emotion, and he applied their findings to music. In a nutshell, he says that what causes an emotional response from humans, generally, is a series of expectations and fulfillments (or nonfulfillments)—or, you might say, a series of actions and consequences. To illustrate what I mean in the sphere of everyday life, let us say a young woman auditions for the lead part in a musical. She has an

[1] Leonard Meyer, *Emotion and Meaning in Music* (Chicago: University of Chicago Press, 1956).

expectation of being either chosen or not chosen for that role from among the candidates who auditioned. There is a period of waiting for the results, filled with expectation. The prospect of not being chosen fills her with the emotion of *fear*. If she gets the good news of the fulfillment that she won the role, she will be filled with the emotion of *joy*. Or if she gets the bad news that she was not chosen, she may be filled with the emotion of *sadness*. However, if the expectations are fulfilled in an unexpected way, she may have a mixture of emotions. For example, if she learns she has been selected to be in the show but is offered a different—though still important—role, she may have both *disappointment* and *gratitude* at once. If she is offered only a bit part in the ensemble with no lines, she may experience both *anger* and *disappointment*. However, if the directors tell her that they did not think she was the right match for this show and then offer her instead the lead in an even better show at a more prestigious theater, then she may be filled with *surprise* and *amazement*, in addition to *rejoicing*.

Music can give analogous signals, according to Meyer. This requires that the music operate according to somewhat consistent principles so that it can set up a "language of expectations". For example, in the musical vocabulary of so-called common practice–style music—that is, traditional tonal music—the "home" chord of the key, called the tonic chord, is used to end almost all pieces of music, providing a feeling of conclusion. There are a limited number of other chords that traditionally precede the home chord and that, acting together with it, have come to signal conclusiveness or give a cue that the music is ending, for most listeners. Because we have this expectation, we may feel fulfilled with the emotion of *satisfaction* when we hear it, or if it is *too* predictable, we may feel *boredom*. If a radically different chord is played by accident (or an obviously wrong note mistakenly played anywhere else, for that matter), we may feel a jolt of *unpleasant surprise*. But if a purposely different but also pleasant chord is played, which takes us into a wonderful new theme in a new key, we may feel a jolt of *delighted surprise*. So, how the expectation is fulfilled, unfulfilled, or fulfilled unexpectedly is the consequence of actions that went before, as cause and effect. This creates for us not only emotion but a kind of language of musical "meaning", according to Meyer.

This system of meaning in music depends upon some familiarity on the part of the listener with what typically happens in a certain style of music. Those who are listening to very progressive jazz for the first time may wonder why the rest of the jazz aficionado audience just applauded, because the new listeners do not "get" the delightful surprise that just happened, relative to that style. In fact, it may sound completely incomprehensible to them. The same might be true regarding the expectations within many musical traditions from other countries, such as traditional Indian music or Balinese gamelan music. It might also be argued that contemporary classical music that is Modernist and atonal fails to speak to many people because it can sound completely random and therefore unpredictable to most ears. By definition, randomness cannot set up any expectations to be either fulfilled or unfulfilled. However, if you set up the expectation throughout this music that it is going to continue in a random way, it would arguably be a meaningful surprise, albeit an odd one, to tack on a traditional ending as described above. (This is exactly the kind of thing with which Postmodern composers purposely decided to experiment. We will return to this in chapter 4.)

Music and the Emotions

Can a piece of music "contain" emotion? Can it be rightly said that such and such a composition is an "emotional" composition? As a composer often accused of writing such pieces, I must say that my commonsense answer is yes, music can contain emotions, but only in a certain sense, or with certain qualifications.

First of all, the term *emotional* when applied to music almost always connotes a weepy, loving, romantic, or sad emotion. One rarely hears that a jubilant-, celebratory-sounding work or an angry-, harsh-sounding work is "emotional", even though jubilation and anger are also emotions. So in the strictest sense, many more pieces of music "contain" emotions than the typical usage of the term *emotional music* implies. Music itself, however, being only tones in the air, does not and cannot *feel* anything itself, because, as I have noted in my introduction, music is not literally a person but only a symbolic reflection of personality.

Let me illustrate this way: When you look into a mirror, you do not see another actual human person but only a reflected image of one. Perhaps the first time you look into a mirror after a major car crash and see your own image terribly battered and bruised, you feel sadness—but the image in the mirror does not feel sadness, or anything else. The emotion is entirely in your response, not the mirror's. The mirror image itself does not "contain" human emotions, only the visual cues or triggers (the bruises) to which you respond with emotion. Likewise, "emotional" music does "contain" a set of triggers, such as harmonic suspensions, minor scales, slow tempos, legato phrasing, melodies with long notes that can be played with lots of vibrato, and so on.

As a composer, I have observed another misunderstanding about emotion in music. After I have written a sad-sounding piece, some people have remarked to me, "That music is so sad! You must have been very sad when you wrote it. What happened?" Susanne K. Langer explains that composers do not "take dictation" of their own emotional states in real time because a piece of music is not written in real time. It may be written over the span of many weeks or months, during which all kinds of personal emotions will come and go. One cannot personally sustain the emotion of a piece for weeks or months. Therefore, composers call upon their knowledge and memory of emotions and can, as a matter of craft, write music with those kinds of triggers though they themselves might be in an entirely different state of mind or mood during some of the days they work on the piece. One of the things the movie *Amadeus* got right was that Mozart wrote some very happy music when he was experiencing the direst and saddest of personal circumstances. He must have remembered how happiness felt from an earlier time. However, Langer says it is not so simplistic as the composer transcribing into music notation his knowledge or memory of "happy" or "sad"; rather, it is a matter of his expressing his more abstract forms of feeling ("feeling" understood more comprehensively, not limited to emotions, as we have said), which may turn out to convey a complex mixture of emotional triggers for the listener.[2] I will return to this momentarily.

What about music that is generally considered "non-emotional", like a fugue by Bach? I would argue that these works do reflect distinct states of mind, even if perhaps "feelings" more than "emotions". For example, a Bach

[2] Langer, *Philosophy in a New Key*, 238.

fugue can have a kind of cerebral serenity or a kind of mathematical sense of rightness and balance that can be very calming to some people. I once knew a woman who was extremely high-strung who claimed she could not listen to Tchaikovsky's very overtly emotional-sounding music because it had too many climaxes and made her too nervous. She could calm her nerves quite nicely, though, with the more even continuity of Bach. (There is a rapidly growing field of *music therapy*, by the way, and several universities offer it as a major. Music therapists on staff at some hospitals, working in coordination with physical and occupational therapists, have learned what kinds of music are helpful to the rehabilitation of Alzheimer's patients, injured children, and people with autism and clinical depression, in particular.)

Let me return to the idea mentioned above of mixing different emotions in music. So far, I have purposely simplified this discussion to imply the conveyance of one emotion at a time. However, in the actual experience of listening to music, there may be a combination of many simultaneous emotions and feeling responses, as in life. The music may convey mixed signals, with the ironic conveyance of two opposite emotions at once or in juxtaposition. (Mahler is famous for this, going suddenly between child-like songs and dark minor harmonies.) The multiplicities of various cues and messages in the music may interfere with one another or pile upon one another in succession so as to collectively result in a *cumulative disposition* (as psychologists call it) that is greater than the sum of its parts, and which therefore can even symbolize transcendence. By that, I mean that as God is above and outside His creation, so can the overall mood or affect of the music seem to hover "outside" the tones. (We will return to this in chapter 7 in a more theological context.) I would speculate that this accounts for the mysterious spirit of strength in the music of Beethoven that speaks so strongly of his distinct musical personality, for which a mere analysis of his harmony and form cannot entirely account.

Rightly Ordering Our Emotional Response to Music

Let us turn to an exploration of the role of emotion—that is, the ordering and disordering of emotion—in the Catholic life, as it relates to music. First, we must secure our terminology by quoting from the *Catechism*:

> The term "passions" refers to the affections or the feelings. By his emotions man intuits the good and suspects evil.
>
> The principal passions are love and hatred, desire and fear, joy, sadness, and anger.
>
> In the passions, as movements of the sensitive appetite, there is neither moral good nor evil. But insofar as they engage reason and will, there is moral good or evil in them.
>
> Emotions and feelings can be taken up in the virtues or perverted by the vices.
>
> The perfection of the moral good consists in man's being moved to the good not only by his will but also by his "heart." (*CCC* 1771–75)

The sentence I want to highlight first in regard to music is this one: "Emotions and feelings can be taken up in the virtues or perverted by the vices." Let us quickly review the seven classic virtues defined by Saint Gregory the Great, along with their corresponding, opposite vices (also called the capital or deadly sins); the four traditional cardinal virtues, derived from the book of Wisdom; and the three theological virtues, derived from Saint Paul's First Letter to the Corinthians (*CCC* 1805–45, 1866).

Four Cardinal Virtues	Three Theological Virtues
Prudence	Faith
Justice	Hope
Fortitude	Love/Charity
Temperance	

Seven Virtues	Seven Deadly Sins
Humility/Modesty	Pride/Arrogance
Generosity/Charity	Avarice/Greed
Kindness/Gratitude	Envy/Jealousy
Patience/Compassion	Wrath/Anger
Chastity/Purity	Lust/Impurity
Temperance/Moderation	Gluttony/Voracity
Diligence/Fervor	Sloth/Laziness

How remarkable that these traits can be so objectively listed and catalogued, as if they were things we could simply choose to do or not to do—but indeed they *can* be done, and we *must* do them, with God's help! How different that is from today's feeling-based, relativistic, situational ethics. Elvis Presley and Louis Armstrong both recorded a song that began, "I believe for every drop of rain that falls, a flower grows." Given how many people speak today in terms of "how I feel" rather than "what I believe", you could well imagine that song being sung today as "I *feel* that for every drop of rain that falls ..." Many today base their life on that same question Pontius Pilate asked Jesus, "Quid est veritas?" (What is truth?; Jn 18:37). A life lived and based upon feelings rather than upon objective truth can easily be disordered. Likewise, if the role of music in one's life is based upon feelings and emotions rather than upon the objectively proper role music should play in one's life or in one's thinking, it is likely to become disordered. If music itself were composed and performed with only emotional preparation and without objectively correct technical preparation on the part of the composer or performer, it would be a disaster. The musician can come out on stage and feel the music with all his heart, but the audience will not be moved if it is poorly composed and played. (I have observed this on some television talent shows. Some people auditioning sing horribly, then throw a tantrum when the judges reject them, because they felt the music so deeply and always dreamed in their heart of winning; after all, isn't the competition based on how deeply sincere is their desire to win?)

Emotions and actions, according to the Church, can be *rightly ordered* or *disordered*. If they are "taken up in the virtues" and not "perverted by the vices", then they are rightly ordered, and vice versa. It is easier to discuss the right and wrong ways *people* use music than it is to say whether and how a piece of instrumental music is intrinsically rightly ordered or disordered. Obviously, songs with words must be judged by their words as well as their music, and that is not our topic in this book. (By the way, a piece of instrumental music is not called a *song* but a *composition* or a *piece*. Music is called a song only if there is a vocalist who sings.)

A piece of music may present symbolic emotional triggers that of themselves are "neither moral[ly] good nor evil", according to the *Catechism* quote above. It is what we do with those emotions that matters. This explains why some music can be fine for some people to listen to and harmful for others to listen to, according to individual conscience and individual weaknesses. For example, someone lacking good Catholic moral formation and who is prone to wallow in misguided understandings of infatuated romantic love may spend hours swooning in a gooey stupor over the ultra-Romantic music of Wagner or Tchaikovsky. But the person whose formation is good, who knows that love's true purpose is "to will the good of another" (*CCC* 1766), may be able to appreciate properly the beauty of that same music and with the right amount of moderation (i.e., with the cardinal virtue of temperance).

Although a piece of vocal music can be said to have intrinsically evil lyrics, can a piece of instrumental music be said to be objectively or intrinsically evil? Some of us might be tempted to speculate that chaotic Modern classical music or heavy metal or acid rock music might appear to come close to being inherently evil as music, even without words, because they seem to convey chaos. And it may well be that some of this music is the product of a confused and disordered human imagination. But we must evaluate a piece of music objectively on its own content, not on the life or motives of the person who created it. (Some very disordered artists have created some very beautiful music.)

In discerning and evaluating emotions in music, a great deal depends on the context of the work. For example, in Shakespeare's *Macbeth*, we are confronted with evil in the form of greedy ambition, lies, and gory murders. However, it is clearly a morality play and a cautionary tale against those vices and sins, and they are discredited rather than glorified in the end. In that context, it is fine for most adults to see that play. In the same way, a piece of music may present some darkness and tension, not as an end in itself, but in the context of its ultimate resolution into a sense of redemption, victory, and beauty later in the composition.

I do believe that some music, lacking such a positive context, may sound like the epitome or very embodiment of ugliness or rage. In fact, I once facetiously told someone in response to a certain piece of atonal classical music, "If I died and woke up in hell, this is the piece of music that would be playing on the jukebox there, for all of eternity." In regard to another endlessly random and grating Modernist piece played at a concert, a friend sitting by me whispered, "This is the soundtrack to slitting my wrists!" At another similar concert, a woman leaned over and whispered to me in all seriousness, "Is this a Halloween concert?" I replied, "No, but in Modern classical music we celebrate Halloween all year round." So it is understandable that we may imagine that certain instrumental music reeks of what sounds to many ordinary folks like evil or some kind of musically dysfunctional distortion.

Such speculation aside, it seems clear that the emotions symbolized by some music may present an *occasion* for sin for some people, *if those people choose to indulge in listening to that music's symbolized emotions in a disordered way*. Notorious mass murderer Charles Manson claimed that it was the Beatles' song "Helter Skelter" that incited him to go out and vent his raging emotions in the act of murder. However, it did not *make* him do it or compel him to do it against his will. Murder was how he chose to respond to it. So we must each consider and discern, personally, what the true moral effect of a piece of music is on our own psyche and choose to listen to it or not, as the Holy Spirit directs us. I will say here again that my comments concern only the instrumental aspects of music. Music with lyrics that promote intrinsic evil is clearly not the ideal choice for a Catholic.

Again regarding the play *Macbeth*, I would further point out that the direst sins are ironically described in very excellent and beautifully wrought English, providing a further context of goodness in which the play's dark events are set. In music, it is also possible to present dark and tense ideas in a beautiful way. To stick with the theme of Shakespeare, Tchaikovsky's pounding, serious music depicting the conflict of the Montagues and Capulets in his *Romeo and Juliet Fantasy Overture* is perfectly sufficient to make its dark point, even in an attractive and traditional style. It is not necessary or required, as some may suppose, to have the instruments create the sound of a plane crashing into a junkyard, or the sounds of weird monsters and cats being tortured, in order to depict this tension. It is quite possible to have plenty of tension and relative dissonance in music without sacrificing beauty, and in my experience tension within the context of beauty usually has more emotional power. (We will come back to the word *beauty* later, since it a controversial word nowadays in some circles.) As with prescription medications, more is not always better. There is some threshold of musical chaos and discord and information overload beyond which most listeners simply tune out.

CHAPTER FOUR

How Music Communicates to the Culture: Contemporary Classical Music

Having discussed the relationship between music and the individual in terms of physics, psychology, and the emotions, we now widen our discussion to the relationship between music and communities or cultures. This chapter is about current classical music, and the next will be about the wider musical culture. I want to encourage even those who do not listen to classical music to read this chapter, because it contains a good deal about the general nature of music and Catholic teaching that should be of interest to all.

The Great Divide between the Public and the World of New Classical Music

I have mentioned in previous chapters Modernist, Postmodernist, atonal, avant-garde, or contemporary classical music—in other words, the music being written for the concert hall by most classical composers today. Because this style of music has become so marginalized in the wider American musical culture, some readers may lack any familiarity at all with it, and so I would ask you to take a few minutes to go online and listen to an example of this kind of music by one of its giants, Elliott Carter (1908–2012), such as his String Quartet no. 3 or his Piano Concerto. Listen to at least a few minutes of the work, if not to all of it, and you will get a sense of the style.

I took an informal, man-on-the-street poll to get a response to the pieces above and got the following feedback: "It sounds like noise." "It makes me feel disturbed." "It is completely ugly. How can anyone want to hear that?" And from an eight-year-old child: "Oh, it hurts my ears!" However, I can assure you that this composer's music is highly celebrated, and Carter has received the highest artistic awards, including two Pulitzer Prizes for Music, two more Pulitzer finalist citations, and the title of Commander in the French Legion of Honor. His works are performed by the greatest orchestras and chamber musicians of the world! What can account for these polar-opposite reactions?

Around the turn of the twentieth century, all the fine arts experienced radical changes, partly in reaction to world events and partly in reaction to what artists perceived as art itself having reached some dead ends in the decades just before. I will leave it to the reader to research more about the history of this Modernist revolution, but for now, it is enough to know that it happened in all the arts. For my informal poll, instead of playing a Carter composition, I could just have well shown many ordinary folks a photo of a celebrated and highly awarded abstract painting and received a roughly comparable negative reaction. However, because people are more used to seeing abstract paintings than they are to hearing "abstract" music, the reactions to the painting might not be quite as visceral. The eight-year-old probably would not have said, "It hurts my eyes!" That is possibly because, unless abstract works in the graphic arts depict horrific or explicit scenes, they at least can be taken simply as colorful design, as you might see on the fabric of a scarf, and they do not grate on the eyes the way music can grate on the ears.

I did not introduce this topic to discuss what is good or bad in art and music, at least for now. It is tempting for us to make simplistic condemnations of anything we do not understand, and I do believe that the Modernist artists were sincerely motivated by the spirit of their age, seeking to reinvent their art. It would be a cheap shot for me to complain about the time I paid a seventeen-dollar admission to the Guggenheim Museum to see some blobs of melted PVC pipe on the floor, so I will not mention it. (I know, I just did.) Rather, what I wish to address here is simply the fact that we are left today with an artistic culture that, as far as I know, has never been more polarized in history—and it has been so since the early to mid-twentieth century. I dare to say that never has high art, or fine art, especially contemporary classical music, been more utterly incomprehensible to the common man.

What strikes me as more than a little ironic is the fact that the intelligentsia, who think of themselves as populists and champions of the poor and downtrodden, are the very people who support and promote music that only a few of the elite can understand. If they were consistent in their principles, one would imagine that they, like the early Soviets or the leftists of the American 1930s, would be championing precisely the opposite: music that "the people" could understand; one would expect them to promote more "fanfares for the common man". I will avoid further political commentary here, but Catholic social teaching indeed tells us that we should be concerned with the dignity and holistic welfare of the poor, including their ability to fully "participate in society", wherein the arts play their part.[1]

I would understand if *non-Christian* artists were mainly concerned, in their work, with their personal expression, no matter how many people like or dislike it. Such artists are not necessarily under any obligation to write music for anyone outside their small circle, if they so choose, and what I say here is not meant to impose such an obligation on them. What I am writing here is for *Christian* artists, Catholics in particular. The non-Christian may well believe that he is doing humanity a service by being "ahead of his time" as a kind of artistic prophet. He may believe that his work will someday be understood and valued by future generations as important to the advancement of society. After all, he might ask, is it not the case that great artists are often misunderstood in their own time? One might object that we have had nearly a hundred years for our ears to "catch up" to the twelve-tone (atonal) method devised by composer Arnold Schoenberg, and the wider culture still has not embraced such music, leading many to question whether it was simply a failed "progressive" experiment. Over the years, I have been to many contemporary music concerts billed as "The Music of the Future", which certainly has an intrigue for the ticket buyer. After all, who wouldn't want to come and find out what the music of the future will sound like? Will it be fundamentally different from the music of the present, and if so, in what ways? (Often, though, such compositions ironically

---

[1] "Seven Themes of Catholic Social Teaching", United States Conference of Catholic Bishops, 2005, http://www.usccb.org/beliefs-and-teachings/what-we-believe/catholic-social-teaching/seven-themes-of-catholic-social-teaching.cfm; cf. Pontifical Council for Justice and Peace, *Compendium of the Social Doctrine of the Church* (Vatican City: Libreria Editrice Vaticana, 2004).

never even make it into the future—they are performed one time and then forgotten.) Yet this discussion leads us to ask: Is everything in art relative, and can music thus do or be anything it likes; or are there instead universal principles that lead a musical composition to become a timeless masterwork instead of a forgotten experiment? This question goes to the very nature of music itself.

Pope Saint John Paul II, in his 1999 *Letter to Artists*, writes of a related gulf or polarization between the contemporary arts and the outside world:

> In the modern era, alongside this Christian humanism which has continued to produce important works of culture and art, another kind of humanism, marked by the absence of God and often by opposition to God, has gradually asserted itself. Such an atmosphere *has sometimes led to a separation of the world of art and the world of faith* [italics mine], at least in the sense that many artists have a diminished interest in religious themes.[2]

In a section of the same letter entitled "The Artist and the Common Good", Saint John Paul mentions the responsibilities of artists to the enrichment of society as a whole:

> Society needs artists, just as it needs scientists, technicians, workers, professional people, witnesses of the faith, teachers, fathers and mothers, who ensure the growth of the person and the development of the community.... Obedient to their inspiration in creating works both worthwhile and beautiful, they not only *enrich the cultural heritage of each nation and of all humanity, but they also render an exceptional social service in favour of the common good* [italics mine].[3]

---

[2] John Paul II, *Letter to Artists* (April 4, 1999), no. 10.
[3] Ibid., no. 4.

Given such a noble calling to contribute to "the common good", I do not know that a committed *Catholic* artist ought intentionally to compose music that only a few of the elite can understand. The disconnect between the general public and the world of academic music may, yet again, have something to do with transcendence and immanence. How so? To begin with, contemporary classical music is, so to speak, written primarily "for the page". Technically, a musical score is not "a piece of music" but a written *plan* for a piece of music, just as a blueprint is not a building but a plan for a building. Technically, we should not say, "Did you remember to bring your music?" or "Hand me that music" when referring to sheet music scores, any more than we would say, "Hand me that building" when referring to a blueprint. Yet one could propose that music may also perhaps exist conceptually or potentially—that is to say, transcendentally—on the score page. This would be something like an affirmative answer to the age-old question, If a tree falls in the forest and no one is around to hear it, does it make a sound? When Beethoven was completely deaf toward the end of his life, he was still able to conceive and notate scores on the page that he would never be able to hear physically. (To be fair, having once been able to hear physically, he was able to imagine and remember the sound of music and "hear" it interiorly.) So we can perhaps say with some confidence that the paper score has a transcendent aspect in and of itself and wholly apart from the music's immanent aspect: the actual sound. The musical score may be discussed conceptually and analyzed in journal articles and in lectures. Over the last few decades, I have read any number of these articles and sat through any number of these lectures. All sorts of formulas of symmetry and organization may be put on a page in graphs and subsequently discussed. (For example, a twelve-tone row may be "combinatorial", for any readers who know the lingo. And apart from serialism, there are many other styles that may be analyzed "on paper" in such cerebral or conceptual ways.) However, in many, if not most, cases these extremely complex relationships are completely impossible to perceive aurally for almost everyone, even for those of us who have studied them and teach them in university courses on historical music theory. The ironic result is that a highly organized work can *sound* utterly random. Within some academic circles, I believe it is the transcendent, conceptual aspect that matters more, not so much how the work in its *immanent* incarnation actually sounds to the uninformed. To some, it simply does not matter as crucially how the music sounds, partly because we have now supposedly moved past the naïve era of "personal expression" and "emotional listening".

It may be helpful to recount my own experience, as a case study. I grew up with tunes floating through my head as a child and eventually sought out the knowledge to commit them to music staff paper. I have clear recollections as a preschooler of hanging upside down from the bars of a backyard swing set and thinking of new melodies. By high school, I was doing arrangements of popular songs for the school pep band and then composed an original march for the concert band. When I attended college as a music theory and composition major, I expected to develop further in writing the only music I knew about, traditional melodic music. Instead, I found myself quickly indoctrinated and acculturated to "the music of our time", as it was euphemistically called. To please my teachers, I began dutifully mastering that style. (A brief aside: "The music of our time" is, in my opinion, a dubious expression, because any style of music written now *is* "of our time", by definition, and itself defines what the music of our time is. However, the phrase may serve to intimidate anyone wanting to use a more traditional style, in order to imply that he is "behind the times".) Within just a few years of earning my doctorate in music composition, I had won just about every national "young composer award" and composition contest that could be won at that age. I was highly decorated, with framed certificates on my wall to show the world, and was now qualified to be a professor of composition. But something was not right.

None of my family or friends cared to hear recordings of my music after it was performed! They could not be called ignorant; they were educated, sophisticated people. Nor honestly did I care to hear my own music. I thought to myself, "If I have no desire to hear my own music again, why should anybody else want to?" and "How is it that hardly anyone likes pieces of music that have won so many important national awards?" I began to want something more. I wanted to write music that had full classical integrity, yes, but that my family, friends, and I could also enjoy hearing, like the classical works I loved by the great composers—the symphonies of Brahms and Tchaikovsky, the piano concertos of Beethoven and Rachmaninoff, and pretty much anything by Ravel. In fact, this was another disconnect. What I was composing sounded nothing at all like what I myself was listening to; they were in entirely separate (perhaps historical) compartments. Interestingly, I was not alone among my peers in this, and I wondered whether this was the first era of music history in which so many composers were writing music that sounded nothing like what they themselves enjoyed hearing. So I came up with a personal mission statement: simply to try to write music that I myself would want to hear if I were sitting in the audience and that conformed to my own tastes *as a listener*—music, moreover, that I and others would want to hear over again many times, like the great works of the standard repertoire.

However, I had been taught at that time, or rather had been warned, that writing that kind of music would be the kiss of death to a career in the concert hall and would have me blackballed from academic circles. If I brought in to my composition lessons any music that sounded even slightly "emotional", my teacher would inform me that it was "schmaltz" and must be removed. It is not nearly so restrictive now in the twenty-first century as it was in the late twentieth in this regard, at least in some universities. Some younger classical composers now have at least theoretically reached a somewhat wider (but still miniscule) audience with somewhat more accessible postmodern styles. It is no longer taboo to aspire to connect with a wider audience. But at least until 1990 (and even to this day in some circles), students were warned that writing traditional music would be regarded as a historical anachronism, artistically disingenuous, pandering, and merely derivative or of a secondary or commercial order. I heard over and over that once the genie of Modernism was out of the bottle, which it was, there was no going back. But I thought, Really? A beautiful tonal melody can *never again* be written in classical music and still be regarded as classical? Even if it is part of a masterfully written composition?

Eventually I found several classical composer role models who did write listenable, melodic music and who did compose after the genie had been released in the first half of the twentieth century: Rachmaninoff, Sibelius, Prokofiev, Vaughan Williams, and a bit later even Barber. None of these composers, although working within a tradition, sounded derivative of the past to me, and all of them sounded very different from each other. Each had a unique artistic voice; moreover, each had an indisputable

excellence of craft. It seemed to me that these composers collectively demonstrated that a more traditional
approach would remain viable for composers in perpe-
tuity, even now. Indeed, the works of these composers
are regularly performed and broadcast today, essentially
outliving the works of many Modernists who were supposed by the intelligentsia of their day to supersede them.
(One might make the same observation about certain tra-
ditionalist painters like Norman Rockwell, whose work
was dismissed by some as kitsch in my youth but now
is esteemed in high circles.) However, while in theory it
did not seem too late to try to add my name to that list
of early twentieth-century greats, I simply had not been
taught how to do it, even with a doctorate in composition,
and reaching such a goal is far easier said than done. Thus
began my twenty-year quest—through self-instruction,
which consisted mostly of trial and error and which largely
took place below the radar—to develop my own well-
crafted, unique, personal, nonderivative, yet listenable
"voice" as a composer.

Let me make clear that I did not invest blood, sweat,
and tears into this steep learning curve, or weather the
backlash from the artistic powers that be, in order merely
to "pander to the audience" and be "liked". Nor did I
"sell out". These were some of the red-herring accusations
that were sometimes leveled in academic circles at anyone
who dared to write music that ordinary people might like.
As I said, I undertook this quest partly for myself, because
I wanted to be able to write music that I myself actually
liked and wanted to hear again as a listener; partly for the
sake of my social consciousness as a Christian, first as a
Protestant and then later as a Catholic; and partly to give
genuine pleasure and joy to the people I knew and loved.
To illustrate this last point: when my father was only days

from death and I placed some headphones on him in the nursing home and let him listen to a recording of one of my new pieces, he said he thought it was beautiful and put on a big smile of enjoyment. Though he no longer knew who I was, he had been a great music lover and appreciated the classics while I was growing up. This was a tremendous joy for me.

You may ask why and how such arcane, abstract music continues to be written and performed. I have mentioned the disconnect between the transcendent, conceptual idea of music on paper and the immanent realization of it in sound, and the supremacy of the former seems still operative for some composers, though increasingly less so. Nonetheless, institutionally speaking, at many universities only faculty composers who have been trained in the prevailing Modern or Postmodern aesthetic are hired and get tenure. They, in turn, choose which students to admit and thus who will eventually get tenure in the next generation, thereby creating a self-perpetuating system. Also, it is possible for a member of any subculture, be it a relatively small religious sect, model-train enthusiasts club, bird-watchers society, or some other group, to surround himself with the magazines and online social media of his organization, to attend all the national conventions and events of the group, and thus convince and delude himself that he is far more mainstream than he really is. It is easy to pass on that delusion to impressionable students, who do not always awaken to how tiny and marginalized a genre Modern classical music really is until after they graduate and no longer have ready, if any, access to those ivy-covered concert halls.

Indeed, at least in America, universities are turning out far more graduates with doctorates in music composition than there are faculty positions for them to acquire. Some

of these graduates go on to become music reviewers and
staff members of performing organizations as a way to
make a living and keep some foot in the culture of Modernist music, as is reflected in many reviews I see, which
are equally out of touch with mainstream culture.

I have discussed why I think composers keep writing
in a style that so few enjoy, but this does not answer the
equally compelling question of why so much of their music
continues to get performed by major orchestras, chamber
groups, and opera companies, when those groups know
very well that most of their audience (and even their own
musicians) will dislike it. An acquaintance of mine who
is a donor to the arts and sits on the boards of two well-
known opera companies recently asked me, with a certain
amount of frustration, why the directors of these companies keep commissioning and performing new operas that
their own internal surveys show are highly disliked by 80
to 95 percent of their audience, which amounts to what
he called a suicide mission for the financially struggling
operatic genre. I replied that one possible reason is that
such organizations depend partly on grants from funding
sources like the National Endowment for the Arts. Often
these grant applications, out of concern for the "future
of the art", require the organization to show what new
works it has commissioned or performed, making sure that
the organization is not just a "repository of the past" (an
epithet commonly used by promoters of new works). If
one major opera company takes a chance by commissioning a new opera from, typically, an established Modernist
symphonic composer, then it appears in the operatic trade
journals, and other opera directors then feel it is "safe" to
perform that opera. Many of these directors know there
will be a certain amount of audience backlash, especially
with so much budget money at stake, and they need to

be able to cite that such and such major opera company previously performed this work and thus prove it is a legitimate or established work of the new repertoire. Often the opera's musical shortcomings are overlooked because of its important topical story or message, lavish sets, and big-name singers. In the case of symphony orchestras, by contrast, the new works are typically kept to tolerably brief durations (six to twelve minutes), paired in the same program with the most popular classical pieces or with standard concertos played by big-name soloists, in order to draw an audience, and often the new works do not even appear on the promotional ads for the concert. Thus the orchestra has done its duty to present new works but without sacrificing its audience.

There has arisen such an expectation that new works will have a Modernist sound that new works in a traditional style are not likely to be taken seriously. We hear sometimes of lost scores by the old masters being discovered in a trunk in some attic and then greatly celebrated. This has caused me to wonder: If such a piece of beautiful, great but lost music from the past were discovered in a trunk, *and if the discoverer succeeded in passing it off as his own new composition*—for example, if it were Debussy's "Clair de lune" or a symphony by Sibelius—would it be accepted and celebrated on its own merits? Or would it be dismissed out of hand with a sniff by some reviewers as "background" music, New Age music, elevator music, or audience-pandering music?

One reason such a piece might be brushed off in this way, I believe, is that some current and former members of this ivory-tower culture have essentially become disordered listeners who can no longer tell the difference between serious, classical, tonal music with counterpoint, modulation, harmonic tension, and form, and the most simplistic, commercial New Age music, which exhibits none of these traits. I have encountered some who, upon hearing a new strongly crafted piece with traditional tonality, have quit listening after only a few bars, tuning it out instantly as simplistic, commercial pabulum for the masses. I believe some would do the same with that piece discovered in the trunk. They seem to have lost the ability to hear harmonic tension within a tonal vocabulary, and find everything about traditional tonality bland, because they have acclimated their ears to only the most extreme dissonance as a representation of harmonic tension, like a hardcore gin drinker who can no longer tell that wine has any alcohol in it.

It is possible that for some, the price of indoctrination into this elite musical culture is a kind of hearing loss or an impatience, inhibiting the simple enjoyment of what the rest of us hear as normal music. Upon the first few seconds of listening to what they think is a new piece, they are immediately searching for some conceptual interest, political commentary, shock or surprise elements, postmodern juxtapositions, and other such features they can discuss with others, rather than for elements of beauty that one can simply enjoy for their own sake. That does not necessarily mean that these souls will no longer listen to and appreciate a piece that they do know was written in the past; however, they have such different expectations for any *new* piece that anything new written in a traditional style, no matter how timeless and well done, represents a kind of disappointment. New music is supposed to have—is absolutely required to have—some sort of, for lack of a better word, gimmick!

I myself did not realize for a long time just how out of touch with and marginalized from the mainstream we academic composers were as a musical demographic, even from the mainstream of classical music. Although there are a few more popular or classically inspired crossover groups emerging now who can draw up to five hundred people at a university concert—for example, the vocal group Roomful of Teeth, which incorporates elements of Tuvan throat singing—the typical new-music performance often has far less than one hundred in attendance, and recordings of this kind of music typically sell less than one hundred copies. By contrast, a young female country music star recently performed on tour in Nashville and sold out the arena of twenty thousand seats for three nights running. The newspaper said indications were that she could have sold it out for five nights. Of course, numbers alone are not a validation of what is better; in some cases, it could even be the opposite. I mean only to demonstrate how remarkable it is that the purveyors of a genre of music so minuscule in size as to be completely unknown to most of the populace can continue to imagine—and convey to students—that it has inherited the mantle of, and is still at the forefront of, mainstream musical progress and culture at large, like a tiny fundamentalist church that truly, honestly believes only its few members possess the real truth. If indeed the train tracks of music history have led us to this point, I prefer to think that this is not the destination but only a temporary passage through a dark tunnel, and the train will once again emerge into the sunshine.

What I am leading to is this: If most such pieces of music are played only once or twice (as they tend to be) for tiny audiences, or even once or twice for larger audiences by symphony orchestras, and no new pieces of music "stick" and come to be regularly performed as part of the standard repertoire, from where will the contribution on behalf of the twentieth and early twenty-first centuries come? I realize that to some minds, the concept of a canon or of

a standard repertoire is outdated. I respectfully disagree.
What if such an attitude had been adopted a few hundred
years ago? We would not have the treasury of our repertoire that we enjoy today: the great symphonies, overtures,
and tone poems of Beethoven, Brahms, Tchaikovsky, and
so many others. For the Catholic composer or musician,
especially, it would seem to be in the interest of "the common good" and an "enrich[ment of] the cultural heritage
of each nation and of all humanity", to quote Saint John
Paul II, that enduring and beloved new works be contributed to the repertoire on an ongoing basis, even as others
may prove more temporary.

Meanwhile, what have Catholic universities been doing
to fill the void? The larger ones, in some cases, are indis-
tinguishable from their secular counterparts; their music
composition faculty may not even be Catholics. Small,
faithful Catholic colleges that do hire mostly Catholic faculty tend to offer only sacred music training and do not
deal directly with these issues. I will write more about this
in chapter 9, because I believe addressing these questions in
their curricula is long overdue.

The Importance of Narrative in Music

So far, I have covered what might be regarded as the more
sociological aspects and problems of much of today's contemporary classical music, from a Catholic perspective, as
well as some of its technical problems: too much complexity to aurally comprehend, a lack of perceivable expectation and fulfillment, an emphasis on things that only
make sense on the written score, and a high level of dissonance, generally. Perhaps the most important element
to add to this list has to do with a sense of narrative in the

composition as a whole—the perception that the music is not merely random and chaotically unpredictable but is telling a story in sound. This element will lead us to explore what specific musical techniques or criteria might instead reflect the good, the true, and the beautiful, which is to say a Christian worldview.

Ordinary people say they dislike much Modernist and Postmodernist music because of its dissonance and harsh cacophony, yet those same listeners have no problem tolerating some very dissonant and chaotic music in movie soundtracks—for example, in battle scenes or intense chase scenes. That is because the film supplies a context and a narrative element that may not be present or evident in the music alone. The same listeners might not find that same music very comprehensible apart from the film. But they can understand music that *does* supply its own sense of narrative without needing a film, as is the case with most traditional classical music. Narrative is that element in music whereby the listener can perceive a musical "story line", like a river with a forward-moving current that pulls you along through time to some sense of dramatic climax or emotional arrival.

In Catholic circles in recent years, there has been a great deal of interest in the idea and the importance of narrative in literature, including the power of fairy tales by such writers as George MacDonald, J. R. R. Tolkien, and C. S. Lewis. Joseph Pearce, in his wonderful 2018 exposition of this topic in *Further Up and Further In: Understanding Narnia*, describes Jesus Christ as the archetypal storyteller, manifested in His use of parables. Pearce explains the importance of narrative in human life:

> To tell stories is merely to tell things as they are. [But] we are not merely *Anthropos*, which in Greek means "he

who looks up"—in wonder (at the stars, for instance); we are also *homo viator*, "man on a journey," the journey of life, with the soul's purpose of getting to heaven. This means that each of our lives should be seen as a quest or a pilgrimage, which can only be understood in terms of a narrative.[4]

That is to say, our own lives actually have a "plot", as a story does, though we may not always recognize it until later. For Pearce, life is not a mere succession of events, in which one thing randomly follows another; rather, life has a purposeful storyline. Certain experiences teach us lessons that lead us to make specific choices we might not have otherwise made. The soul, according to Pearce, moves from purpose to purpose, as if on the road to an end goal—like a long pilgrimage to heaven. So when we say that life has a "narrative" character, we mean that a narrator could recount our lives as he would a story, with a setting, a conflict, a beginning, a middle, and an end. Because of this, we can identify with and respond sympathetically to parables, fictional stories, and, likewise, music that symbolizes a narrative flow toward some point of "arrival".

How exactly might narrative appear in music? While in popular vocal music and hymns the lyrics typically convey the most obvious sense of narrative, over a repetitious tune—though even there, the harmonic progression usually also pulls the ear forward—the great instrumental music, particularly in longer movements of twelve to fifteen minutes' duration, can contain even more compelling and powerful narratives, too deep for words. Acting

---

[4]Joseph Pearce, *Further Up and Further In: Understanding Narnia* (Charlotte, N.C.: TAN Books, 2018), 28.

with all the mystery and magic of a fairy tale, such music can pull the ear along through new lands. The listener becomes a *homo viator* on a sonic journey.

A very basic and obvious example of narrative music is found in the 1940 Disney film *Fantasia*, in the beloved "Sorcerer's Apprentice", where Mickey Mouse plays the title role. The narrative of that scene depicts Mickey trying his hand at magic after the sorcerer has gone to bed. He animates a broom to sprout arms and carry in buckets of water, so that it will do his chores for him while he takes it easy. Things get out of hand, though, and the broom begins to divide and multiply so that a whole army of magic brooms eventually carries in too many buckets of water and creates a flood indoors, until the master sorcerer finally awakens and puts things right. This is the arc of the visual film, but the music, by itself, also supports this narrative interpretation, beginning relatively serene then gradually spiraling out to swirling and wild orchestrations of the main theme. In fact, this was indeed a standalone classical piece, *L'apprenti sorcier*, written in 1897 by the French composer Paul Dukas (1865–1935).[5] It functioned independently as a concert favorite for forty-three years before its eventual use in *Fantasia*. I cannot think of a classical work that better illustrates a sense of narrative, except perhaps for Ravel's *Bolero*. You may wish at this point to go online and revisit the "Sorcerer's Apprentice" from

[5] Dukas was a teacher of one of my first, then very elderly, composition teachers, David Van Vactor (1906–1994). The latter also had studied in his own youth with Arnold Schoenberg, just as one of my other teachers, Ross Lee Finney (1906–1997) had studied with Schoenberg's fellow atonalist Alban Berg. Thus I have two of the seminal fathers of atonality at the "grandfather" level of my training. Other of my teachers had studied with the famous French Modernists Olivier Messiaen and Arthur Honegger, all of whom in my circles constitute a kind of imprimatur on one's résumé, in the master-apprentice lineage.

Fantasia, but only listen to it and do not watch Mickey's interpretation. Notice how the music grows and carries you along to a climactic arrival. Now that you are really listening attentively without multitasking, you can easily hear the narrative element. This is an important lesson: with most classical music, only by giving it one's full attention does one notice or fully experience the narrative. Yes, you can also enjoy a piece on some level as background music, and that can be fine too—but it is paying attention to the narrative that lets you be swept up into the work's musical "story".

Narrative music, to use another metaphor, makes a sort of "dramatic argument", in which its themes are like the characters in a play who dialogue with one another and undergo transformations, so that by the end of the piece you see (i.e., hear) them in a different way. Two things in music that make us perceive a sense of narrative are the linear thread of a melody and the underlying harmonic progression that pulls us toward the home chord of the key. But there is something more required. In *L'apprenti sorcier*, what drives the story is the way the tune is orchestrated: with progressively more and more instruments, higher volume, and quicker tempo, getting varied and altered and folded in upon itself in echoes of itself, thus increasing the tension and the complexity of the texture. In other words, what builds the narrative is the *development* of the melody and harmony.

We have seen that narrative in music (as in literature or film) can symbolize a sense of purpose and movement toward a goal. After all, Christians believe that their lives have been given a specific orientation: to grow in holiness here on earth and ultimately enter eternal life in heaven. But when one hears nonteleological music (i.e., music with no goal or strong sense of narrative), such hopeful symbolism is absent. For me, this music often seems to symbolize, instead, aimless, confused wandering. I do not mean to say that narrative, or the lack thereof, must always be a dogmatic criterion for determining whether music is "Christian"; nor am I saying that nonbelievers cannot also find meaning in the purposefulness that narrative can symbolize. However, as stated above, in many contexts narrative can certainly be interpreted by the Christian as symbolic of his journey toward heaven. Of course, not all music is completely narrative or completely nonnarrative, black or white. Some music is somewhere between those two extremes. It is possible, somewhere in the middle of that spectrum, for one person to perceive little or no narrative and for another person to be able to perceive in the same piece at least enough narrative to symbolize some forward motion toward a goal. In other words, this kind of symbolism may be detected by one listener and not another, and so we are glad the Church allows for different tastes and perceptions of art—provided the work in question promotes no intrinsic evil—leaving the matter to prudential judgment, on the part of both the artist and the listener or viewer.

But how can an ordinary person, not trained in music, discern the presence or absence of narrative? Fortunately, that is easy: If you can hear the music pulling you forward in time and leading you onward, and if you are inclined to wait to turn it off until it arrives at a moment of closure, then you have perceived some degree of narrative. And if it sounds mostly random to you, and you feel you could just as well arbitrarily turn it off at any point in the piece, then you are not perceiving much narrative.

I would like to point out, however, that some rather chaotic Modernist works, although not having narrative, do have "shape". Still, shape—for example, a gradual increase in volume—does not necessarily equate to a dramatic "climax". In drama, climax entails characters coming to grips with a conflict, and so, for an audience to perceive a climax, they must be able to recognize these characters in the scene. In *L'apprenti sorcier*, for example, the principal melody is a kind of memorable musical "character" one can hear introduced at the beginning and then continue to recognize throughout, even though it develops into an increasingly wild musical arrangement at the work's climax. But in some Modernist works, like much music composed with Schoenberg's twelve-tone method, there is no memorable musical theme or element at all, no character that can be recognized as transforming or developing toward a truly affecting and meaningful dramatic climax; instead, there is only a "growing louder".

In all fairness, it may take a couple of hearings to register that such transformation is taking place, so we should give more challenging and complex pieces of music, even those in a traditional style, a fair chance. For example, it may take a few more hearings to fully follow the narrative in Beethoven's late string quartets than it does to perceive the narrative in *L'apprenti sorcier*. By the same token, in a piece that immediately reveals its narrative, you may well, upon a second hearing, perceive "subplots" in the music that had previously gone undetected, and you will likely be further enriched by listening to it yet again.

As I have stated, the presence or absence of narrative in music is not an absolute litmus test for whether that music exhibits a Christian aesthetic. Neither is narrative the sole element in music that can symbolize a Christian worldview. For example, Gregorian chant does not have a strong sense of climax or narrative, but it does have other wonderful features that I will discuss in chapters 7 and 8.

Let us explore some other criteria for discerning Christian symbolism in instrumental classical music.

Discerning the Transcendentals in Music

One obvious set of criteria for the Catholic to measure anything by would be the formula of "beauty, truth, and goodness". So much has been written about these three *transcendentals*, as they are called, that I will not attempt a comprehensive treatment here. Let us examine, though, how they might apply to the realm of music.

Truth and *goodness* are of supreme importance in vocal music (songs), specifically the lyrics, but in instrumental music, they are more ineffable, more elusive, tougher to pin down, at least simply by hearing them. However, already a sense that a piece of music has some structural and formal coherence might symbolize a kind of rightness, to start. A study of music theory will reveal that this formal coherence and rightness we sense intuitively in the great works of music go beyond just a feeling. While introductory music theory for students deals with rudimentary matters like scales, keys, and harmony, more advanced studies in music theory reveal a far more complex coherency in musical design than we might have imagined. For example, Austrian music theorist Heinrich Schenker (1868–1935) showed, among other things, how great works of music may be analyzed in "levels" of background, middle ground, and foreground, each with its own hierarchical tonal structure, in which "cells" of music reproduce or project themselves on each level according to different time frames. The results are practically biological, analogous to the way human cells with their DNA reproduce themselves into tissue, then organs, then organ systems, and finally whole organisms.[6] The American theorist Fred Lerdahl (b. 1943), working with linguist Ray Jackendoff (b. 1945), showed us in his "generative theory" how something analogous to the above-mentioned "cell reproduction" happens through rhythmic organization on different "levels" of time, exhibiting characteristics of a kind of linguistic grammar and syntax.[7] These and other advanced studies essentially provide empirical evidence that what we intuit as rightness in the form of music is due to many properties analogous to the organization and symmetries found in natural creation. I believe that if the organization of creation can be said to represent "truth", so can great works of music represent truth, or at least a reflection of that truth.

As a teacher of university music theory classes for many years, I have often spoken of the "architecture" of a piece of music, suggesting that the design of a skyscraper, too, represents a kind of truth, in the simple fact that it must be designed in harmony with the laws of gravity and physics in order not to fall down. All the more "true" would be Filippo Brunelleschi's brilliant design for the Florence Cathedral, home to the largest cupola, or dome, in the world, which defies gravity in still-breathtaking ways. So does the famous self-supporting staircase of the Loretto Chapel in Santa Fe, New Mexico. Sometimes, as in the case of breathtaking music, "truths" can be not merely true but truly wondrous.

But can the natural creation, and by extension things like music and architecture that reflect it, also be "good"?

---

[6] Heinrich Schenker, *Free Composition* (Hillsdale, N.Y.: Pendragon Press, 2001).

[7] Fred Lerdahl and Ray Jackendoff, *A Generative Theory of Tonal Music* (Cambridge, Mass.: MIT Press, 1996).

In the words of Genesis, "And God saw everything that he had made, and behold, it was very good" (1:31)—so, yes! Two key words in this verse are *behold* and *very*. *Behold* enhances the sense of God's wonder before his own creation, the world. The word *very* strengthens the phrase: it was not merely good, ho hum, but extremely and wondrously good—behold! When we consider further that God did not have to create anything at all but chose to do so, ex nihilo, out of nothing, and purely out of love, the goodness of His creation is undeniable. As with truth, music and art can partake in this extravagant goodness. A musical composition, for example, might exhibit a certain patient charity toward its listeners by offering them easily recognizable themes to hang on to, richness of color and texture, and pleasant moments of resolution, instead of just imposing the artist's own raw personal expression.

Now we approach the fine line between something truly good and wondrous and something of "beauty", our third transcendental. But before crossing it, I must answer a question that might be asked about certain highly structured atonal or Modernist compositions—for example, music using serialism or the twelve-tone method. Since that music, too, has a strong structural design, can it not also be said to be true and good? I have said above that in the great works of traditional music, we sense or intuit (and in many cases clearly hear) that a formal design is at work, and analysis by theorists serves to illuminate exactly what that audible formal design is. In chapter 2 (on the psychology of perception), I pointed out that in the case of twelve-tone music, the formal structure is unfortunately so complex or information-overloaded that, ironically, we cannot aurally sense or intuit anything but randomness, and in some cases also chaos and disagreeable dissonance. (Cancerous cells can also be said to have a structure, but this is understood as a disordered structure, because of its effects.) So, even if an analysis of such music does convey some truth on paper, that message of truth is not conveyed in sound, which is the principal way that music is consumed.

As for "beauty", I would like to say that one of my own goals as a composer has always been to try to leave the world a more beautiful place than I found it. Wouldn't we all wish to do that, no matter what our profession? *Beauty* can be a slippery term to define, though. I have just suggested that perhaps it flows from, or is our reaction to, the wondrousness of truth and goodness. This goes hand in hand with my earlier suggestion that the evidence for the existence of God given by Saint Paul in Romans 1, the evidence of the creation itself, is compelling (or should be, he says), not only due to our cool recognition that it evinces an intelligent structure, but also due to our awe and marvel at its beauty. Therefore, I propose that fully recognizing beauty also, ideally, involves a component of gratitude, humility, and awe. I will not attempt here any kind of comprehensive discourse on beauty, which others have provided in abundance, but rather offer an ingenuous affirmation of beauty's existence. During my university studies, the simple term *beauty* was so philosophically deconstructed and approached with such relativism that it was rendered entirely subjective and therefore unusable and irrelevant to any credible aesthetic position or statement. The term was simply dismissed as naïve. After all— the thinking went—beauty is in the eye of the beholder, so nothing can be said to be ugly, especially if doing so might seem uncharitable to those who like the musical work in question. If nothing can be ugly, then nothing can be beautiful, or everything can be beautiful, and so the word becomes meaningless.

Nonetheless, as Catholics, we are left with the fact, mysterious and juridically unprovable though it may be, that as a matter of natural law the inner human person, possessing a sound mind, can somehow innately recognize beauty when encountering it. When seeing an elegant ballroom dance by Fred Astaire, most people instinctively know that it is beautiful, though it may be impossible to explain why. All the more, people know that a field of wildflowers on a mountaintop on a spring morning is beautiful, or that a fresh mountain brook splashing over rocks is beautiful, though this beauty cannot be technically proved. As an artist, I finally learned simply to trust in this innate sense that people have, though it is a mystery I cannot understand. If academics cannot define beauty, so what? Some things in the world simply resist explanation, and convoluted attempts to explain beauty away defy common sense.

Yet I will concede to academe that what people generally regard as "beautiful music" is probably too narrowly understood. The term conjures up in many minds only music that is slow, serene, and gentle, with a lyrical melody, like the slow movement (second movement) of Mozart's Piano Concerto no. 21 in C, K. 467, famous for its use in the 1967 film *Elvira Madigan*. But the livelier first and third movements of the concerto could be called beautiful too. Just as the wind on a shimmering lake can be beautiful, so can a shimmering Sousa march. Just as a blazing sunset can be beautiful, so can a blazing, fast composition, like the third movement of Beethoven's Piano Sonata no. 23, nicknamed the *Appassionata*; so can the "Russian Dance" movement in Tchaikovsky's *Nutcracker* ballet.

Catholics can at least confidently say that things that depict intrinsic evil are definitely not intrinsically beautiful. The murders in *Macbeth*, of themselves, are not beautiful, though they may be described with beautiful poetry and be enwrapped in an overall message of moral goodness, since the play is a cautionary tale. We use discernment to sort out what is and is not beautiful in a context of truth and goodness. In the case of abstract instrumental music, such discernment is admittedly more difficult, but not so relativistic as to be completely impossible. We will return to the theme of discernment in chapters 5 and 6. For now, suffice it to say that while there can be such a thing as acquired tastes, the visceral reaction of common people to music, as a matter of natural law, is generally reliable. If the music sounds harshly ugly to normal, rational people, and if children and animals recoil from it, I think one can safely call it ugly, or at least not beautiful. Most mature adults outside academe can see through the convoluted, relativist arguments used to convince impressionable students that two plus two does not always equal four, that trees falling in the forest make no sound, and that ugly music is beautiful to someone somewhere and therefore no beauty is possible for anyone and the word *beauty* must be banned forever. In short, I am saying that beauty is not "in the eye of the beholder". A beautiful thing is beautiful in objective fact, whether or not someone likes it. There are great works of music that are not to my personal taste, but I can acknowledge that they are beautiful.

Another element in music that a listener might examine is that of human communication, or lack thereof. In some Modernist circles, the ideas of personal expression and communication are, like beauty, considered naïve, a product of obsolete nineteenth-century thinking. For them, the music simply exists on its own, and it is only the listener who *imagines* that it is communicating to him. But the Christian tradition from its earliest years has used art to communicate, be it through iconography-rich frescoes, splendid cathedral spires, or Latin antiphons sung with expressive melody; with these, even the illiterate could depend on a kind of "Scripture" to read from.

If music can communicate, then perhaps it can also convince. In *The Art of Rhetoric*, Aristotle outlines three "appeals"—qualities necessary to persuade someone in an argument or speech: ethos, logos, and pathos. Ethos is the credibility of the speaker—or in the case of the composer or performer, a convincing skill or mastery of the craft. Logos is a logical and well-structured argument, or in this case a perceivable musical narrative, as discussed above. Pathos is an appeal to the emotions of the hearer, which might be analogous to the emotional component of music discussed in chapter 3. (An example of pathos: When in a speech we hear "I have a dream!" we are more emotionally moved and persuaded than if the speaker had proclaimed, "I have the following three-point plan!") Music, too, makes its "appeal" and can "persuade" us with these same three elements—or fail to persuade us, if they are lacking.

What about the issue of consonance and dissonance in music? In the preceding discussion, I have been careful to suggest that dissonance is not necessarily the most important factor in why Modernist music is problematic for many people, yet it remains an issue nonetheless. A student of mine taking a developmental psychology class recently sent me a scientific study about very young infants' perception of consonant and dissonant intervals (i.e., pairs of musical tones with different pitches that, traditionally speaking, can produce either harmony or discord when played together).[8] It concluded with what

[8] Marcel R. Zentner and Jerome Kagan, "Infants' Perception of Consonance and Dissonance in Music", *Infant Behavior and Development* 21, no. 3 (1998): 483–92, https://www.sciencedirect.com/science/article/pii/S0163638398900212.

has been obvious to most folks since the time of Pythagoras: humans are innately pleased by consonance and
innately displeased by dissonance. The ancient Greek
mathematician Pythagoras is credited with showing that
two vibrating strings whose lengths are in simple proportion to each other (such as 1:2, 2:3, or 3:4) produce two
pitches that make a consonant interval, which indeed
is true. But he went on to say that these most simple,
natural, and pleasing proportions also reflect the respec-
tive distances of the seven known planets from the earth,
and that each planet produces a tone, pitched the same
as the aforementioned strings, though the sound of this
"cosmic music" is too exquisite to be heard by ordinary
ears: it is the "harmony of the spheres". While the latter statements are certainly fanciful, academics in music
also often dismiss his fully reasonable view that consonances are more pleasing. They maintain this first of all
because consonance alone, as they rightly recognize, can
be boring. In fact, it is rather the interplay of dissonance
and consonance, of tension and resolution, that creates a
kind of "language" of meaning—and thus an interest—in
music. However, what some in academe have ironically
failed to recognize is that unrelenting dissonance can also
be boring, or at least essentially static, and can get tuned
out by listeners for the very same reason they might
tune out perpetual consonance: a lack of meaningful
interplay. (Technically speaking, there are still relative
consonances and dissonances in Modernist pieces, but
the level of contrast between them is often too subtle to
perceive.) Thus, the overall level of dissonance in fully
chromatic, so-called aggregate-driven, atonal music often
crosses a threshold into meaningless displeasure for many
listeners, even for those like me who have studied and
analyzed it in music theory classes at the doctoral level,

taught it in college classes for years, and ought—if anyone can—to be pleased by it.

The concept that consonances are innately more pleasing
is dismissed, second, because many assume that a displeasure with dissonance is not innate ("nature") but learned
("nurture") and that people must simply be educated to
discord, unlearning this biased preference. Granted, up to
a point, there is, as I have said, such a thing as an acquired
taste, with food as much as art, and up to a point some
greater dissonance can become palatable. However, a presumption of consonance as a kind of baseline for musical language—as the study on infants attests—is arguably
supported by nature and not only by nurture. That is to
say, musicians and theoreticians have long considered
that dissonance seeks resolution in consonance—not the
reverse—and this belief is by no means without scientific
foundation.[9]

Third, the Pythagorean idea is rejected with an aesthetic
argument: even if some music is ugly, art is not always
meant to be pretty and nice. In principle, I agree. Art may
also portray very dark things and even purposely confront
the audience with discomfort. One need think only of the
William Golding novel (and its film adaptation) *Lord of the
Flies* or the brutal tragedies of Sophocles, like *Oedipus Rex*.
I have mentioned already that it is still possible to present
ugliness in a beautiful style. Now, if the artist's intention is

---

[9] Notes high in the overtone series with mathematically more complex frequency ratios (dissonances) are more complex for the brain to process, as compared with low overtones with simple frequency ratios (consonances), such
that the motion (resolution) from complexity to simplicity represents a kind
of equilibrium or relaxation from tension in the brain's perception, just as the
proportion 100:200 is more instantly understandable than, say, the nearby but
more complex 100.003:200.004 (which the brain tends to "resolve" by round-
ing it off or, in music, "tuning it up" to the former).

merely to disturb with more extreme cacophony, so be it, and let people who wish to be so disturbed be disturbed; it's a free country, as the saying goes. But artists, please do not make those who do not wish to get quite so unnerved, or for quite so long, feel like second-class artistic citizens. Some people lead disturbing lives to begin with and, like the troubled King Saul, look to music for respite. In my opinion, this argument against traditional beauty also fails to take into consideration the problem of time. Whereas an unsightly painting in a museum can be viewed in its entirety at once, and the viewer has the freedom either to turn away or to continue looking, a piece of music in its entirety unfolds only through time, and concertgoers are a captive audience: it is awkward to get up and leave from the middle of the row when the saturation point of distur-bance is reached. For many listeners sitting there suffering, this seems to send a condescending or paternalistic message from the stage: "You are not going to leave this table. You are going to sit there and eat your vegetables, because we know better than you, and we say that they are good for you, and you'll thank us later! Besides, it was announced before we played it that this is a masterpiece, so if you don't like it, it's your fault."

Postmodernism in Music

Let us turn to Postmodernism in music. The term is a bit slippery to define. First, it has a literal definition, in the strictly chronological sense of being after Modern-ism. Here, *modern* is understood not in the generic sense of "contemporary" but as a specific cultural movement during the first half of the twentieth century, with an uppercase *M*. Postmodernism emerged in music during the last forty years of the twentieth century (though the word had been used much earlier in visual art as a reference to works made after French Impressionism.) Second, Postmodernism can be defined as working *in reaction to or in contradistinction to* the principles of Modernism. However, whereas other famous musical "isms" are associated with a particular musical style, Postmodernism in music encompasses several musical styles, more or less united by a common philosophy. Indeed, pluralism in style is one of its key traits. What Postmodernists do all have in common is an attitude of irony, relativism, and skepticism toward belief—belief especially in traditional notions of narrative, whether a grand historical one or an isolated musical one. The early twentieth-century Modernist Arnold Schoenberg, for example, still clung to the idea that he, in his turn, was the heir to the flow of progress in musical style through music history, just as Beethoven had been. Schoenberg's music did aspire to unity and a narrative flow, even if it was too complex for many to follow. In short, it was music that still believed in itself. Postmodern music, by contrast, is often full of eclectic references to all kinds of music within the same composition and does not see itself as belonging to some inevitable historical flow. In music, Postmodernism also tends toward greater populism, distancing itself from dissonance and musical elitism and embracing more consonant styles, even if they do not form a traditional narrative.

Living through much of this movement myself as a professional composer, I have observed that the form it has taken has expressed the desire on the part of some composers to bridge the gap with the alienated audience that I have described. By creating collages that quote bits of tonal, traditional music, often from the standard repertoire or even from popular music, these postmodern composers provide the ears of listeners with something more accessible to latch on to and enjoy. It honestly does not seem to me to have succeeded in increasing the size of the audience one bit, but in my estimation they have at least given the ones who were already there a great deal more entertainment. With the much earlier precedent set by composer Charles Ives, George Crumb (b. 1929) was among the first of those with a high profile in America to employ quotations with a postmodern sensibility, like using bits of Franz Schubert's "Death and the Maiden" in his work *Black Angels*. Composers like William Bolcom (one of my teachers) and then several composers in my own, younger generation brought the collage style to its apex, often referencing popular culture, with Michael Daugherty, for example, writing a symphony based on the comic-book hero Superman.

Audiences have found these works more fun to hear in the concert hall, but the fact that recording sales for them are as tiny as ever indicates a fundamental problem. For listeners, it is perhaps enough to hear these pieces one time as a sort of novelty and then move on. To me, the fact that listeners do not care whether they hear any of this music— Modernist or Postmodernist—a second time, that they do not fall in love with it and want to hear it for the rest of their lives like perhaps they did with Rimsky-Korsakov's *Scheherazade* or Ravel's *Pavane for a Dead Princess*, is the proverbial elephant in the room among these artistic circles. The music often turns out to be as disposable as the worst of forgotten pop music. Yes, it has succeeded in being a little more accessible to the ear, but at what cost? As with Postmodernism in general, this music seems to be "art about art" rather than "art about life". When we hear a bit of something beautiful, it tends to be brief, quickly interrupted by something else and framed by a kind of "wink and nod" from one sophisticate to another, who both get the irony. For me personally, this represents a crisis of faith, because the listener becomes self-conscious of the references and cannot believe in the music or enter vicariously into any drama. The spell of a narrative keeps getting broken by abrupt shifts to other things, much as it does when there is an aside from the stage in a play or when, as in the movie *Braveheart*, a car can be seen accidentally left parked in the background of a fourteenth-century horseback battle scene. I sit in the concert and think, "Now he's quoting this; now he's quoting that." The harshest critics claim that in Postmodernism, the great works have become a mere storehouse of material to be exploited by parasites who have no real ideas of their own, for often, the only parts of these compositions the audience actually enjoys are the parts written by someone else. I myself have likened some postmodern concerts to curiosity shops filled with fascinating novelties. But as with a visit to Ripley's Believe It or Not!, however entertaining it might be to hear these pieces once, most people do not need to go back a second time.

In this milieu, there arose other experiments that can be broadly called postmodern, some more successful than others. For instance, there are the hypnotic, repetitive, and generally consonant strains of minimalism (e.g., music by Philip Glass or Steve Reich), which for me tend more toward Eastern meditation than narrative. This kind of music employs extended repetitions of a short pattern of tones for as long as thirty minutes or more in a kind of meditative stream, seldom and only slightly changing. There is also postminimalism (e.g., music by John Adams), which introduces more frequent changes, giving a greater sense of narrative to the repetitive, but more colorfully textured, structure. Then there have emerged experiments

by a variety of composers with using world-music influ-
ences in a minimalist or collage setting (e.g., "Ansa Ya" by
Merrill Garbus, recorded by the group Roomful of Teeth).
Finally, we have postgenre music, which is essentially an
even more chock-full (and at times incomprehensible)
collage of rock, pop, and atonal classical styles, with an
emphasis on musical crossovers between rock and classical
music performed in nontraditional venues like art galler-
ies and rock clubs (e.g., the composition "Future Shock"
by William Brittelle, one of postgenre's foremost expo-
nents and, incidentally, a former undergraduate student of
mine). Mannes School of Music in New York now offers
a minor in postgenre creation and performance.

Among these styles, there may be found some examples
of new classical music that, while not conforming to traditional melodic, narrative styles and perhaps even being
born of Modernism or Postmodernism, many traditional
and religious listeners find nourishing—for example, the
ethereal, slow, and relatively consonant minimalist works
of Arvo Pärt (b. 1935), Henryk Górecki (pronounced
Go-RET-ski; 1933–2010), John Tavener (1941–2013), and
James McMillan (b. 1959), all composers of openly Catholic or Orthodox faith. There is a liturgically influenced,
chantlike sensibility in many of these works, contribut-
ing to their appeal as havens of peace or contemplation
in sound. There are a number of other composers in this
vein active today, and it seems likely there will be more
to come.

Is A Return to Tradition Possible Now?

Now I will mention my own music for the concert hall.
I do so only because, being in a truly traditional style, it

raises the question of whether neotraditional music can possibly be genuine or rather must necessarily be considered a disingenuous anachronism, like a skillful forgery of a great painting. The same may be asked about certain painters today who have most skillfully recaptured a traditional representational painting technique. Are we legitimately putting back on the tracks a train in music history that was derailed early in the twentieth century (even earlier for painting), or are we rather trying in vain to put a genie back into his bottle, which can never be done?

One clue might be found in the late nineteenth century. Brahms' two great clarinet-viola sonatas, op. 120, and Dvořák's equally Romantic *Humoresques* for piano, op. 101, were written the same year as Claude Debussy's groundbreaking proto-Modern *Prelude to the Afternoon of a Faun*, 1894. One might say that the day of Brahms and Dvořák at that point had already passed, that their music was literally passé. But from our vantage point now, these distinctions have become irrelevant. I have never heard these works mentioned less favorably than Debussy's. Few are even aware now that they were composed at the same time. What matters to listeners is that all the works are intrinsically great and have a unique and personal, rather than merely derivative, style.

The fundamental aesthetic question here is this: How do we evaluate works of art? Is their worth encapsulated by the historic context in which they were created, or do they transcend time because of their intrinsic and universal qualities? I believe that although the two Brahms sonatas mentioned above are to some extent a product of their age, which accounts for the musical language of their style, their deeper, intrinsic, internal coherence is self-authenticating. Their value is thus timeless and universal. They would be just as great if they were written now, and the presence of the artist's unique voice and spirit would still be felt "between the lines". This is another form of transcendence in music. The Passion and Resurrection of Jesus Christ took place, similarly, at a particular point in time and space but exists universally, outside of time, as we will see in chapter 7. In the Mass, the faithful reach outside the temporal sphere and re-present the event of Christ's death just the same as it occurred in the first century. Analogously, so it is with music. The misunderstanding about music history—that traditional form and consonance are definitely behind us—perhaps comes from likening the arts to science or medicine. Medicine has clearly improved with time, so medical treatment is objectively better now than it was in the past. We now have antibiotics, for instance, instead of leeches. The same goes for sciences like chemistry, biology, and physics. Music history, on the other hand, while marked by innovations and improvements in the instruments and greater variety in harmony, does not simply "improve" over time. A beautiful aria from the Baroque is not necessarily "worse" than a beautiful aria from the later Romantic era. What matters in music is the composition's universal and timeless qualities, or lack thereof, no matter when it was written.

Rather than *old* and *new*, I prefer to speak of music as either *timeless* or *fashionable*. A newly written composition can be either, or both, or neither. My goal is to write music that has timeless qualities rather than music that meets the fashion of the day. Without meaning to be uncharitable to the dead, I confess that I am old enough now to have known a good number of big-shot, prize-winning composers—imposing and intimidating figures—who are now deceased. During their lifetime, they wrote primarily for other composers, that is, according to fashion and expectation, and now unfortunately their work has died along with them. Their music was mostly performed by musicians whom they knew, who took part in their cult of personality, or who simply wanted to garner some importance by association. Now both the composers and their sophisticated circle have passed on, and in some cases, there is practically no one left who wants to play their music— and even fewer who care to hear it *on its own merits*. Yet the phrases "new music" and "the music of our time" are often used in contemporary classical music circles to refer to new classical music in a Modern or Postmodern style. In my experience and observation, there is often a clear intention to imply to students that if they do not toe the party line and do not write in an approved (Modern-enough) style, they are somehow behind the times or not new. I must argue that whatever someone writes today *is* the music of our time, literally, because it was just written! The music itself defines what is of our time, not someone else's tastes. I often ask my students: If I take a fresh croissant out of the oven, even though made with an old, classic recipe, is it not still new food? Is it not the food of our time? Would you refuse to eat it just because the recipe was old? The croissant itself is fresh and new, made with newly grown wheat! So it is with a new piece of music in a classic style. It is new because *you* are new, and there is no one in the past, present, or future who would write it exactly the way you did. What matters is whether it is well written.

When I began to compose traditional-style music, I had not decided to be "retro" for its own sake, to make any kind of statement, or to recapture nostalgically and naïvely the feel of music I liked from the past. My only aesthetic decision was to seek excellence and mastery of universal and timeless musical qualities, such as narrative, and to imbue my work with beauty. To put it more bluntly, my only goal was to write a good piece of music in my own voice. It is my hope that in another hundred years my works might fare like those of Brahms, Dvořák, and Debussy, mentioned above. No one cares when it was written, only whether it is good and whether they like it or are in some way enriched and ennobled by it.

In conclusion, let me clarify that all the proposed criteria above for discerning transcendental values are meant only as useful tools, not as absolute prescriptions or proscriptions to be applied legalistically. Nor by any means do they constitute an exhaustive list. Rather, they indicate a few examples of the kinds of symbolism and issues that Christians can keep in mind as they listen to music. Astute readers may think of other ways that music can present symbolic representations of these transcendentals generally and in particular moments of particular pieces of music. As a professor, I like to think of the latter as a wonderful term paper or thesis topic waiting to be chosen.

CHAPTER FIVE

How Music Communicates to the Culture: Contemporary Popular Music

Now we turn to music in the wider world and the role it can or should play in the Christian life, both for the listener and the musician. It is hard to talk about today's music apart from the ways it functions in society. For example, I do not personally know anyone who listens to a recording of a marching band while eating dinner at home, to Gregorian chant performed by monks during a football halftime show, to a rock band at a somber funeral, to a Jamaican steel drum group at an Oktoberfest, or to the "Wedding March" at the gym (unless one is hearing Felix Mendelssohn's incidental music for *A Midsummer Night's Dream*, op. 61, from which it comes). Performers value some music just as much for the way it functions as their "vehicle" (a loud, high, impressive ending that will get big applause) as for the quality of the music itself—if not more. Likewise, many of us would agree that such music may indeed be better suited for a showy vocal display than for an instrumental version played in an elevator, where the actual mediocrity of the melody is revealed. And some popular songs are so linked with a particular performer or group that they just would not sound right sung by anyone else, much less played in an arrangement for, say, clarinet and piano. Music in society is often inextricably shared or communal (e.g., the national anthem at a sporting event) in established ways and bound up in all kinds of cultural traditions.

Music now plays over loudspeakers in stores (purportedly in order to manipulate our shopping moods), at county fairs, in doctors' offices, and in restaurants, as well as over the telephone receiver when a business employee has put you on hold. It forms the soundtrack to our lives, so much so that sometimes it is hard to escape its constant bombardment. I cannot help but wonder to what extent we become desensitized to all this music and simply tune it out. Some of us are so used to having it in the background that the skill of giving it our undivided attention has been lost. As one whose whole life has been devoted to music, and as a Catholic, I see a certain irony in this. Music, this beloved gift from God, which should ideally draw us more into a contemplative mentality and thus closer to God, has become for some people a detriment to contemplation and in some cases a raucous distraction from God, even a force pulling them away from Him, perhaps due to its worldly associations and perhaps even due to idolatry, whether of performers or of music itself.

The Lure of Musical Fame

The twenty-first century has brought in the era of the television talent contest. Literally thousands of young people line up outside audition halls, waiting their turn and openly giving voice to their naïve hopes, fragile dreams, and blind ambitions. Most of these youth are just having a bit of fun, but a few of the cases we see on these shows are troubling. Some state outright on these shows that an honest profession in the work world holds no attraction for them; their one and only dream is "to make it" and be famous. They will settle for nothing less than fame, and who can blame them? They have been bombarded since childhood—even by their teachers—with messages along the lines of "You can be whatever you want to be, if you only believe in yourself! Don't let anyone stand in the way of your dreams!" (We might rightly modify these messages to read something like, "By God's grace and with prayer and trust in His perfect will and timing, you can work hard to be the very best you can be, and do what you were truly called to do, for the glory of God.") For some on these shows, it all comes crashing down when the judges tell them what none of their friends have had the courage to tell them all along: that they sing off-key and have no vocal talent whatsoever. Some cannot bear this very public reality check and throw a tantrum in front of the judges for millions of voyeuristic viewers to see, gaining a kind of instant fame they had not bargained for.

This is only a recent example of music's potential spiritual danger. Already more than a century ago, the world knew opera divas, "rock star" performers like pianist Franz Liszt and violinist Niccolò Paganini, and the early musical theater stars. This was followed by the advent of the microphone and of broadcasting that could reach millions instead of only a theater full of people. With this, the idea of the famous musician began to take on great force in Western culture, and many a soul, chasing her siren song, has crashed upon the rocky shoals of egoism, fame, self-idolatry (or should I say "*American Idol*-atry"), and in some tragic cases, self-destruction through dependence on drugs or even through suicide. As I wrote in my introduction, God's creation is good, but it can be ordered or disordered, depending on how it is used. Many popular music genres can be wonderful—even wonderful to pursue as a career and they can be used by God in all kinds of ways, if the music is well ordered and certain potential pitfalls are avoided.

Helping Children Discern Musical Values

How do we help our children navigate these waters? The world bombards them with messages celebrating quick success as a famous performer, equipped with their own social media presence and "publicity" photos. The first generation to have professional-quality, computerized advertising graphics at its fingertips can now create a virtual personal ad campaign to garner "followers" and "fans" and "likes". I think that most kids can discern that this is an illusion, and if they participate in it, it is perhaps mostly harmless fun. But just to be safe, it is good to discuss the issue with them. If they want to learn to play an instrument or sing, parents and teachers should stress to them that doing so ought to be about the beauty of music, not "all about them", and be for God's glory, not their own. (In some cases, ambitious parents themselves might need to be reminded of this.) It could be good to give them a prayer to say before practicing, something like what Catholics say before meals: "Bless me, O Lord, and this, Your gift of music, that I am about to receive. May it be an offering of praise to You, for Your glory, through Christ our Lord. Amen." There is also a lovely excerpt from the prayer to Saint Cecilia (patron saint of musicians): "Dear Saint Cecilia, inspire us as musicians to gladden the hearts of people by filling the air with God's gift of music and reminding them of the Divine Musician who created all beauty. Amen." I know some Catholic school music teachers who have their music students pray this prayer as a group before each rehearsal.

If a child wants to take up music, some discernment and discretion on the part of the parents will prove helpful. For less spiritually mature kids, instruments of the school band or orchestra might be less risky than, say, the electric guitar. It would be harder to get caught up in one's ego as a tuba player than as an electric guitarist, since there are no real tuba superstars selling millions of recordings. In the band or orchestra, children will learn several life skills: working under an authority figure in obedience; working in cooperation with others toward a common goal; setting weekly and long-range goals; discipline, from daily practice; and accountability, to a private teacher or conductor and fellow players. Students will also experience the gratification of seeing their hard work pay off in the progress made.

Let us compare the inherent differences between singing and playing an instrument. Statistically, a relatively large percentage of people—up to 20 percent of all people by some accounts—are blessed with a pleasant singing voice, due to the configuration and size of their vocal chords, larynx, and nasal cavities. Almost everyone can learn to sing on pitch and sound better than he thought possible—and of course, not all styles of popular music even require a pleasing sound at all (in blues, for instance, a raspy sound may actually be an advantage). Obviously, not everyone with a naturally good voice decides to pursue a career in vocal music, but in theory, these people always remain potential singers. Whatever the true percentage of potential professional singers is, it is surely a great deal higher than the potential percentage of people who are likely to study for the many years it takes to master, say, the violin at a professional level. While it takes years indeed to learn to sing on a professional opera stage, it takes a relatively short time to learn to sing popular songs. Therefore, given this high proportion of potentially good singers in the general populace, along with the relative lack of formation necessary to perform popular styles, anyone aspiring to sing modern popular music as a career is surely going to have a great many people to compete with, so he had better have a backup plan! By comparison, the percentage of good viola players one might have to compete with to earn a living as a violist would be far smaller.

Ask your young person: How many popular singing stars do you think "make it" at any given time and become household names? How many can you name? A hundred? Two hundred? Three hundred? Whatever the number, the simple fact is that there are today many thousands of young people vying for one of those relatively few spots, many of whom, when asked, have no backup profession in mind. They have put all their eggs into one basket. They busy themselves making demo recordings, developing their image, and spreading their self-published PR materials, seeing role models to quick fame and success on TV and the Internet. Some even seem to feel entitled to success, as we see in the fits thrown at talent competitions. I would tell young people that popular music is fine to pursue as a hobby, but it makes sense to train for a good "plan B" job they would enjoy doing too. They might also find an opportunity to use their vocal gifts in any number of school and church choirs, with the same benefits of ensemble participation mentioned for instrumentalists above. Someone with a really beautiful voice who serves as a cantor and occasional soloist may not gain fame and riches on earth, but with the right spirit of humility, he can be a true blessing to the Church and will surely have a reward waiting in heaven. The parable of the talents comes to mind (Mt 25:14–30): there are, on the one hand, those who invest the master's gift for the greater good and, on the other, those who, embittered by the master's apparent stinginess, bury the gift altogether for themselves. Do not think that if you cannot be famous, you cannot use your gift at all.

In this regard, it is illuminating to note how far music making in America has transformed, over the course of a century, from an intentionally amateur pursuit to one dominated by a "wannabe" (aspiring professional) mentality. Gerald Carson reports that in 1886, 70 percent of American public school students were taught to read music, and in 1905 there were more pianos and organs in America than bathtubs![1] Prior to recorded music (not to mention television), people had to make their own musical entertainment at home. It was typical for one or more members of a family to be able to play the piano while the rest gathered around and sang. Sheet music sales for home use were commensurately high. For example, two million copies of the sheet music for George M. Cohan's 1917 patriotic song "Over There" had been sold by the end of World War I (i.e., in only about a year's time),[2] and presumably the song itself was played in two million homes. One might safely speculate that only a very small percentage of the people who played or sang the piece imagined that this would be their ticket to stardom. They simply enjoyed performing it as amateurs, for a hobby. The word *amateur* is taken from French, in which it has

[1] Gerald Carson, "The Piano in the Parlor", *American Heritage* 17, no. 1 (December 1965), https://www.americanheritage.com/content/piano-parlor.
[2] "Over There", Library of Congress, 2002, https://www.loc.gov/item/ihas .200000015.

the meaning "lover of", someone who does something for the love of it. Today, in my observation, the last vestiges of that truly amateur American musical culture are preserved not so much in homes as in the old-style houses of worship across the land, with their manifold gospel quartets, volunteer choirs, and unpaid performance groups of every kind.

In terms of young peoples' listening habits, much guidance is also needed from parents and teachers. There is perhaps nothing more challenging and frustrating to teen-aged Christians than popular songs with great melodies—with which they fall instantly in love—and immoral lyrics that they know are wrong. To these young listeners, I suggest using your own creativity to invent a whole new set of good lyrics to sing with these melodies, using your own guitar or keyboard. But for a parent, more practicable would be trying to replace these songs in the child's consciousness with something even better. Children tend to have a very small "reserve" of music in their mental musical repertoire. To broaden this, parents can take them to ballets, musical theater shows, and concerts that expand their vision and give them many more (superior) choices.

The classroom, too, can be an important source of formation. My wife, a K–8 music teacher in a Catholic school, collaborated with me to develop a method by which children can learn to discern values in music, which she has successfully been applying in the classroom for the last few years. In appendix D I have condensed some of the content of her PowerPoint slides. These slides involve the seven virtues and discussing how they apply to the study and performance of music. Readers who teach music are welcome to adapt these freely and make their own set of slides to use in the classroom. Appendix E shows a "Virtue Rating for Songs" handout we developed, originally presented in the form of a PowerPoint slide. This is a form students fill out as a homework assignment, analyzing a song of their choice. During subsequent classes, each student brings in a recording of his song, plays it for the class, and presents his findings. The other students can then discuss the song and offer further input.

Beauty as "Pre-evangelization"

We have seen that music is not only a personal affair but a profoundly communal one, just like our faith, which gets passed to the next generation through careful spiritual formation. Although the culture tends to use music as a commodity that shouts at us at every turn, the Catholic should take care that he not become desensitized to its beauty and contemplative potential, or to its potential to enrich, bless, do good, and draw people to God. With regard to this last capacity, the beauty of music can be a tool of what might be called "pre-evangelization". If we spread beauty wherever we go, if we live lives of beauty, and if friends see our lives adorned by a love of beautiful music instead of all things stressful, crude, and vulgar in music, others may be mysteriously drawn to us and our friendship. If they see Christ in our love of them and of God's beauty, some may also be drawn to desire the beautiful, mysterious peace we possess in Christ.

CHAPTER SIX

HOW MUSIC COMMUNICATES
TO THE SPIRITUAL SOUL

We must dig deeper—beyond science, psychology, and sociology—into spiritual truth as it concerns music. Note that it is not my intention here to go into all that has been argued regarding whether *spirit* and *soul* are synonyms for the same thing or instead indicate two separate things, a topic much debated in Protestant circles.[1] From this point on I will employ the term used most often in the *Catechism* (e.g., *CCC* 366), *spiritual soul*. The spiritual soul is the "innermost aspect of man" (*CCC* 363), which has been summed up by some as the mind, will, and emotions, and by others as memory, intellect, and will. We might consider it as synonymous with the biblical term *heart* (*CCC* 368). Finally, as I explained in my introductory remarks on the Real Presence, the *Catechism* affirms that in this life, the human body and spiritual soul are essentially united in substance at conception to make a person (*CCC* 364). Remember that while music imbues the matter of

[1] The *Catechism of the Catholic Church* indicates that in Scripture, the words *spirit* and *soul* are sometimes used interchangeably but sometimes used separately, even in the same verse, to refer to different aspects of the inner person (*CCC* 363–68). The Church teaches that "this distinction does not introduce a duality into the soul" (*CCC* 367).

sound waves with *symbols* of personality, its *substance*—air particles—remains only matter. Music can be a compelling *reflection* of a person, but like in a mirror or a hologram, it is only an image and not a real person itself.

All human persons, Christian or not, have been granted a certain amount of spiritual discernment, sometimes called "common grace" by Protestants and "natural law" by Catholics. For example, anyone with an open and healthy mind can know innately that murder is wrong. Romans 1 informs us that at least the existence of God should be evident to anyone who observes the natural creation. In my opinion, such a discernment of God's existence from creation would reasonably seem to be due, at least in part, to the beauty of the creation and not only to its scientific ordering. The heart, including the emotions, is touched by this beauty and plays a role in whether a person "decides for or against God" (*CCC* 368). The natural man's innate ability to recognize obvious beauty can play a role in preparing his heart for hearing the gospel of Christ.

As Christians, our understanding is further illuminated by the indwelling of the Holy Spirit. Christ said of the Holy Spirit: "He will teach you all things, and bring to your remembrance all that I have said to you" (Jn 14:26). Broadly speaking, this is generally understood to mean that Christians' consciences—if they are unhindered by sin and have the right interior attitude or disposition—are now capable, through the Church's teaching, of being "formed" to discern correctly the moral good from evil and the more virtuous from the less virtuous (see *CCC* 1776–1802). Such discernment can certainly be applied to choices made in listening to music, as we have said. It can also be applied to choices made in *creating* music as a composer or in "re-creating" it as a performer. Let us, then, turn our attention to creativity before reflecting on the listener.

Creativity, Spiritually Understood

What is creativity, exactly? If humans are made "in the image of God" (Gen 1:27), and if God is the supreme Creator, it would be no surprise if we were created to want to create things ourselves too, in our own way. Human creativity does not have to be in the arts. It might take the form of placing flowers pleasingly into a vase, arranging pieces of furniture to your own taste in a room, cooking, inventing a gadget, writing a letter decorated with a sticker, sewing, making jam, arranging tools in the garage to hang from an ingenious kind of rack, or any of the other little things people do imaginatively or with care, the things they take satisfaction in doing. In other words, everyone is probably much more creative than he gives himself credit for. I believe not only that humans, by nature, are all creative in some way but that they cannot help but be so, any more than a pear tree can help but produce pears. Not only are we all capable of creativity, but we are all compelled by an innate impulse to create, whether we think we want to, whether we regard ourselves as creative, whether we are even aware that what we are doing has a creative aspect to it, or whether we just take it for granted as "no big deal". It *is* a big deal, when you think about it. That is to say, spiritually, it is quite profound indeed that we have been wired this way by our Creator.

We are told in the first two chapters of Genesis that Adam and Eve were put into the Garden of Eden not merely to sit around and look at it but "to till it and keep it" (Gen 2:15). Instead of naming the animals Himself, God asked

Adam to think of names for all the animals, from his own imagination (Gen 2:19). How much fun that must have been! And when Eve was created, He told them both, "Be fruitful and multiply, and fill the earth and subdue it" (Gen 1:28). Bearing new human children and raising them are both creative acts, and while I have never had the opportunity to "subdue" the entire earth, I know that just tending to my own yard and landscaping requires a certain amount of creativity.

Perhaps it is because we live in a fallen world that we forget about this creative purposefulness we innately should be enjoying. If you have ever taken a psychology class, you might recall learning about Abraham Maslow's "hierarchy of needs", from his 1943 paper "A Theory of Human Motivation".[2] I believe it is fair to say that his ideas accurately describe the situation of people in a fallen world, *not* God's ideal order or the original conditions of Adam and Eve prior to the Fall. He states that people have needs that must be satisfied in the following order: (1) bodily sustenance, like food, water, clothing, and shelter; (2) safety, like not being in danger of death from wild animals or war; (3) some kind of social acceptance or love in a group, as in a family or community; (4) esteem, to be respected by someone else and by themselves; and (5) "self-actualization", a realization of their full potential, which can be expressed in creativity or in any sort of vocation. In his later years, Maslow added a sixth, even higher, need, for "self-transcendence", which is the giving of oneself to something higher or beyond oneself, like God, spirituality, or service to some greater need of humanity.

<hr>

[2] Abraham H. Maslow, "A Theory of Human Motivation", *Psychological Review* 50, no. 4 (1943): 370–96.

By *hierarchy*, he means that the first conditions must be met in order to enjoy the later ones. In other words, it is hard to sit around and dabble joyously with your watercolors when you are hungry, or a lion is chasing you, or your city is plagued by war, or you feel hated and bullied by others. Now let me write an updated version of that sentence: It is hard to sit around and dabble joyously with your watercolors when you work fifty hours a week and commute in rush-hour traffic; when you have to heat up frozen dinners while you calm screaming children; and when, after putting them to bed, you sit down in total exhaustion and catch your favorite TV show before collapsing into bed yourself—and then do it all over again the next day. It is hard indeed, yet this is a picture of the everyday lives of many in modern society. No wonder we do not feel as creative as we were made to be! It is beyond the scope of this book to provide a remedy for such a lifestyle, nor do I wish to offer quick platitudes and admonitions to slow down. I am only accounting for why, perhaps, we do not always feel as creative as we could be.

Perhaps, then, we can conclude that people are often asking the wrong questions about creativity. The question is not whether you are creative but whether, when the opportunity to be creative does arise, you use your innate creativity with gratitude and an understanding of God's role in it. The question is not whether you will impress others or make money from your creative work (you probably will not) but whether you will remain open to the Holy Spirit instead of letting your ego shut out and "quench" (1 Thess 5:19) Him, making it impossible to create as a whole human person. This leads us to define creativity, ideally, as *an imaginative act of the whole human person, both body and spiritual soul, in the grateful humility of one who wants and knows himself to be a vessel of God, and following the Holy Spirit's illuminating guidance with well-formed discernment.*

How Can We Be God's Vessel When Making Music?

All the terms in the definition of creativity have been previously explained except for *vessel*. The word *vessel*, indicating a container (usually for liquid or grain), is used in many Scripture verses with the sense of something or someone that "contains" God's purposes and benefits in order to "pour them out" upon others. There are (depending on the Bible translation) vessels of sanctification, vessels of honor, vessels of lofty use, vessels of mercy, and so on (see Prov 25:4; Acts 9:15; 2 Tim 2:21). I have often heard the term used more casually by Christians who are in the performing arts; sometimes before a performance I hear a small group of them routinely pray, "Lord, make us your vessels." This raises questions for those unfamiliar with this phraseology: What would they, as vessels, be carrying? How does one go about becoming a vessel? Is a vessel something you should pray for God to make you into? And how does one go about "pouring out" the vessel's contents upon others?

The concrete realities of a vessel can give us some insight into the metaphor's deeper spiritual implications. First, a vessel must be *empty* before it can be filled. Thus, when praying before some moment of creativity, we might rightly say something like this: "Lord, forgive my sins and empty me of selfish desires and vanity; empty me of jealousy of other performers, of pride of life, of fear and insecurity, distractedness, and self-sufficiency."

Figure 8: Ancient vessels.

Then we might ask God specifically for what we want our vessel to be filled with; for example: "Lord, fill me with your love for the people who will watch and hear me perform; fill me with peace and all the other fruits of the Holy Spirit, a clear mind, and a spirit of humility and gratitude for the gifts you have given me."

Second, each vessel is *unique* and pours out its contents in a unique way. In the days of handmade clay pottery, no two pots were exactly alike (see fig. 8). At the market, people in biblical times would choose the right container for the purpose, one for water, another for wine, another for grain. Similarly, Saint Paul became a "chosen vessel" to bring God's word to the Gentiles (Acts 9:15),[3] presumably elected because he had the particular experiences,

[3] King James Version.

personality, eloquence, and holiness to do best the particular job at hand. This point about the vessel's unique-
ness leads to an important distinction between *vessels* and
channels. I wonder whether sometimes performers, when
ready to pour out their own contents upon others, mis-
guidedly hope to become channels rather than vessels;
the two are slightly different. Consider the telephone,
a type of channel or conduit by which you receive calls
and messages: it does not conceive or create the messages
itself but only passes on directly what it receives from a
satellite or landline. A garden hose is a channel through
which water flows; the hose does not generate the water.
In popular New Age usage, a medium "channels" spirits
from beyond the grave without any personality or ideas
of his own, acting simply as a kind of human loudspeaker
in real time, sometimes even talking in the voice of the
spirit supposedly communicating through him. This is
not what it means to be a vessel. Though we are God's
ambassadors and are indwelled and energized by the Holy
Spirit, we do not "channel" God when composing or performing music. Nor were the Gospel and epistle writers
(or, for that matter, any biblical authors) mere channels.
They were chosen vessels, because God used their own
particular personalities and writing styles to communicate
His inspired and inerrant Word (*CCC* 106). Luke's style
is very different from John's, for example. They were not
mere stenographers but allowed their own one-of-a-kind
personalities to be perfectly used by God.

Along this same line, vessels have a third property
worth mentioning. They hold on to what they contain.
A channel like a garden hose flows immediately; before
pouring out its contents, it does not fill up, retain the
load, and get carried around the way a watering can—a
vessel—does. While God's gifts are in you, His vessel, they

in a sense become yours and are used uniquely by you. The quintessential vessel, of course, is the Blessed Virgin Mary. Her virginal conception was entirely the work of the Holy Spirit, and her body contained God Himself for nine months; yet even though this was God's own work, Jesus was also physically "the son of Mary" (Mk 6:3), just as much as he was the son of the Most High. Given all this, I turn to the musical performers of today, particularly singers, and advise them to acknowledge that they, as vessels, are distinct from other vessels. Singers, no one else in the world sounds, or is supposed to sound, exactly like you, so kindly stop comparing yourself to other singers. God wants to use who *you* are. How, you might ask, does a musician go about pouring out his contents upon the audience? I believe that this is something you cannot do yourself but rather something that God does! Your job is just to go out there, ideally having been "emptied" of self with a clear conscience and then "filled" with grace, and give the best performance you can, trusting God to use it in hearts as He sees fit.

We also need to examine this topic of creativity from the other side of the music stand, that is, in regard to composition, my own primary occupation. Our situation is very different from that of performers, because we do not compose in real time. We may take many weeks to compose a piece of music that lasts only ten or fifteen minutes when played. To be sure, as much as we may talk about what inspired us to compose the piece, we are *not* inspired in the same theological sense as the Gospel writers mentioned above, because we are not conveyers of divine revelation like the children of Fatima were. Nor do we go to a mountaintop and receive carved tablets of music. Nor are we channels, or stenographers taking dictation from either God or "the universe". If we were, our music would come out perfectly on the first draft, and we would not have to revise it over and over until we think it is the best it can be. Composing is a craft, like writing prose or like designing and carving rocking chairs, all of which take practice.

Some of the notions people have about composers are quite romanticized. The often-quoted account of Handel comes to mind, when he reportedly said the following about composing his *Messiah* in a fervor of divine inspiration: "I did think I did see all Heaven before me, and the great God Himself seated on His throne, with his Company of Angels." At the risk of deromanticizing and demythologizing a beloved musical work, I will inform you that the texts for this famous oratorio were conceived and assembled not by Handel but by the librettist Charles Jennens. Handel was an astute businessman and knew that the English people had a taste for religious works (he was in England at the time), so he set Jennens' text to some new music, as well as a great deal of music rearranged from several of his secular Italian love songs, written twenty years prior. For example, his song "Nò, di voi non vo' fidarmi" (containing the line, "No, I will never trust you, blind love, cruel beauty") was given the new text, "For unto us a child is born." Of course, the final version of *Messiah* is no less great for all this, but the idea that it was somehow inspired by a vision of God was more a matter of good PR than of authentic experience.

I will say, however, that while not having the benefit of direct personal revelation, a seasoned composer does, after several decades of composing music, gain a surer hand that can sometimes feel deceptively like "divine inspiration". His skills have been honed over so many years that there is a sense of just what notes should come next to fulfill the objectives of the work, without thinking or revising as much. Techniques have been internalized. To illustrate what I mean by *internalized*, I could point out that when first learning to type, you probably had to say out loud "A–S–D–F" as you tapped with the fingers of your left hand on the home keys, but later you internalized this knowledge so that you no longer had to think consciously of each letter and key. Similarly, with music composition, you can eventually work much more quickly and know more precisely what you want to "say" in a piece, because you have internalized the techniques used in putting it on the page without thinking about the methodology itself. I no longer have to ponder where B-flat is on a staff or wonder how the oboe will balance with the flute in a certain register; I know these things instinctively. I have learned to hear them in my imagination, simply by having heard them so many times with my ears in the concert hall. I do not need to struggle over artistic choices that were agonizing decades ago; the results now are both quicker and better. One can observe something similar in any master of a trade. I marvel at how a master pizza chef can throw a spinning disk of dough high up in the air and catch it with his fists, how a sketch artist can dash out a perfect likeness of someone in a matter of minutes, and how a skilled assembly line worker can turn out a hundred units in the same amount of time it would take me to turn out five.

So where does God come into this equation, and in what sense can a Christian composer be God's vessel? Like the performer, the composer should ideally have striven to empty himself of all that is wrong and sinful and then have allowed himself to be filled with all that is good, just as anyone should do to be God's vessel in any pursuit. But filling a blank page with notes entails a thousand technical choices, and these choices ought to be guided by, and ultimately reflect, a well-considered aesthetic philosophy.

I believe it is the Christian composer's duty to develop and cultivate a mission statement for his work. If he brings to his work an undisciplined or random imagination with no Christian formation or guiding philosophy, it is less likely that his work will be usable by God as an instrument to draw people to Himself, though the work might appear clever, skillful, or entertaining to the world. Just as performer-vessels are unique, so too composer-vessels are one of a kind and, ideally, will not write music that sounds like an exact clone of the music of someone else. Rather, the composer's work will present to the listener his personal artistic voice, his distinctively imagined "forms of music", which elicit the listener's "forms of feeling" to relay an overall message of beauty, truth, and goodness. How? For example, using inner discernment (whether formed by natural law or by divine illumination), the listener might derive from such music a sense of mental wellness, logic, and peace—the mark of God—rather than chaos, confusion, or dysfunctional disturbance of the spirit—the mark of darkness.[4] This kind of spiritual discernment is famously outlined by Saint Ignatius of Loyola in his *Spiritual Exercises*, as "Rules for the Discernment of Spirits",[5] which the reader may easily find through many online resources.

Listening with the Spiritual Soul

The previous paragraph finally makes a first allusion to how music communicates to the spiritual soul of the *listener*. We have dealt with the performer's and the composer's roles

---

[4] Yes, in some special cases art is purposely meant to disturb us, and I address this and similar issues in chapter 4, on contemporary classical music.

[5] *Spiritual Exercises*, nos. 313–36.

in this communication, which is the first side of the equation. Now let us consider the listener's role in receiving
this communication. In my chapter on music and emotions
(chap. 3), I listed several types of listeners or ways of listening to music from the standpoint of human emotions.
With regard to the spiritual soul too, there are different types of listeners and ways of listening to music. For
example, some listeners, even Christians, enter so much
into the music that it becomes an essentially godless and
hedonistic activity. I am not advocating, of course, that
one must think to oneself, "Praise the Lord!" every thirty
seconds over the course of a symphony. *Sanctified listening*
(listening with spiritual discernment in a state of grace) can
still include enjoying and focusing on the sheer sensual
beauty of music's sound and logical flow and the God-
given talent of the persons who created and performed it.
As with the analytical kind of listener mentioned earlier,
who critiques everything, there is certainly a type of spiritual listening that can discern errors in the performance
with a charitable spirit, but I also have known those who
welcome these errors as fuel for the fire or grist for the
mill of a bitter, critical, jealous, or otherwise uncharitable
spirit. Likewise, the "brand" listener (who chooses music
in order to identify with a certain culture or group) can
regard his brand as mere fodder for a holier-than-thou attitude. When attending concerts of my own music, I have
noticed a difference between those in Europe and those in
the United States. In Europe, live classical music is often a
family activity, attended by working-class people as much
as by the wealthy, while in the United States there can
sometimes prevail a sense of class consciousness: exclu-
sive parties with wine and cheese for tuxedo-clad donors,
where the wealthy or cultural elite can see and be seen,
and even older children are often left home. Music of any

genre can become a tool that people use to differentiate themselves from—and perhaps put down—others, even whole groups. But fundamentally, music is God's gift, not an instrument to appropriate for one's own agenda, whatever it may be.

What, then, should we listen for in music, in order to listen spiritually? Chapter 4 already explored the dimensions of narrative and dramatic argument in music; here we will examine further criteria. Putting aside the question of song lyrics (which must be evaluated on their own), we can, first, try to discern through prayer and self-examination what effect a particular kind or piece of music is having or has had on our spiritual soul upon or after hearing it, as I mentioned in chapter 3 on emotions. In the "Rules for the Discernment of Spirits", mentioned above, Saint Ignatius gives advice on how to interpret and handle the states of *consolation* (cheerfulness, gratitude, peace, etc.) and *desolation* (agitation, anxiety, depression, fear, etc.). Interestingly, for him, desolation might also include feelings of shallowness, emptiness, or debasement, into which some kinds of deceptively happy music (e.g., certain dance and party music) can often draw us down. By contrast, one biblical example of music's consoling function may be seen in 1 Samuel 16:23, when David takes up the harp to soothe the agitated spirit of King Saul.

Here are some questions you might ask yourself when discerning: Does listening to certain music make me feel peaceful, or excited in a cheerful way, or inspired in a noble and spiritually victorious way? Or does it rather elicit in me a sense of stress or anger, or else a kind of wallowing in self-indulgence or self-absorption? Does it seem to take me to, for lack of a better word, a dark place? If this latter is the case, is this sense of darkness part of a narrative that ultimately resolves into something good, or does it fail to resolve, leaving me troubled and anxious or simply distant in some way from God?

There is also the "Can I take Jesus with me?" test. I heard this as a young person from an old and wise Protestant preacher, and it still works for me as an adult. He said, "If you are trying to decide which movie to see, ask yourself if you would be comfortable inviting Jesus to attend with you and sit in the seat beside you." As a Catholic, I have heard the same test framed (by Mother Angelica, I think) as, "Could you take your guardian angel with you?" These tests work for movies (perhaps aided by ratings systems and good Christian reviews), and they can work for a Puccini opera or a Rodgers and Hammerstein show as well. Even though, truth be told, I do not tend to picture our Lord sitting around in theaters and audiences of any kind, I do imagine He would prefer to attend some venues with me more than others. Take, for example, *Les Misérables*. While it may not be perfect in every respect, there is a wonderfully redemptive story in both the book and the Broadway show, and consistent with this, there is also beauty and thrilling consolation for me (as Ignatius would say) in the *music* of the show. So yes, I would be happy to take both Jesus and my guardian angel to it. I would even pay for their tickets. On the other hand, I cannot say I would feel comfortable taking them to see the James Bond film *Goldfinger*, with its gratuitous seductions and unnecessarily graphic violence, even though I find the music and the gadgetry entertaining, and even though it might appear to present a narrative of good winning over evil. At the end of the day, it is a kind of junk food. (Surely the reader can think of some musical equivalent to *Goldfinger* in his own life.)

Of course, these criteria may yield different results for different people, even in regard to the same piece of music.

Any music lacking an obviously sinful message tends to be a matter of individual prudential judgment or, as a Protestant might say, falls within the realm of "Christian liberty".

Deepening Our Listening Skills and Repertoire

From my perspective, our modern culture is, by the standards of previous centuries, overbalanced with vocal music, in the form of popular songs. Some people's only exposure to instrumental music is in films, where it usually serves as a secondary element. Often, after such people hear one of my instrumental compositions, they remark how well it would work in a certain movie. Some people do not realize that instrumental music is alive and well, independent of the cinematic world, with a long history and tradition in its own right before the invention of film. They are unaware that some composers have no desire to collaborate with or subordinate their work to what is on a screen—they are unconcerned about getting rich in Hollywood because their true vocation is in the concert hall.

This phenomenon of associating instrumental music with films is a symptom of a larger problem. Due to the overwhelming diffusion of our current commercial music culture, many listeners do not recognize that they listen in a mode oriented almost exclusively toward vocal music in the particular repetitive form of pop songs. For them, music without singing is almost not music at all, and more demanding pieces are unappealing. In pop music, there is an essentially repetitive—what musicians call *strophic*—structure: stanzas of words (the verse and the chorus) sung to iterations of the same tunes. By contrast, most instrumental, classical music requires more work and attention on the part of the listener. It usually includes melodic tunes, yes, but there are also transitional and developmental passages that can seem boring to people used to hearing mostly just the tune. As chapter 4 argued, it takes more of a road map to follow the form of classical pieces through their unfolding narratives, but with attentive listening, it is generally not that difficult to follow them. Ordinary people have done it for centuries.

Some people tell me that they are afraid they will not know where or how to begin exploring the treasures of the classical concert repertoire. Often the names of the compositions, composers, and performers are foreign and hard to pronounce. But I am unabashedly proposing that some great, spiritually uplifting, contemplative, and thrilling experiences await the Christian who explores these artistic riches. For this purpose, in appendix A at the back of this book, I have provided a short list of suggested classical compositions for the beginning listener, guaranteed to be enjoyable, beautiful, and excellent as great art, as well as edifying to the mind and spiritual soul. This list is meant not to denigrate popular songs but to encourage the addition of some great instrumental music into a more balanced and nutritious listening diet.

CHAPTER SEVEN

THE IMMANENCE AND TRANSCENDENCE OF MUSIC IN WORSHIP

Our View of Time versus God's

I believe that one of the most fundamental intellectual misunderstandings in my life, leading me to theological errors, was to imagine that time works as man sees it instead of as God sees it. By man's reckoning, the Crucifixion happened at a single point in time on a Friday, and the Resurrection happened later, at a single point in time on Sunday. It seemed to me that the Crucifixion, while of course necessary as the great sacrifice for sin, was in a way superseded and surpassed by Christ's subsequent victory over sin and death, the Resurrection. That was why we Protestants did not have crucifixes in our churches; we had only empty crosses. Upon seeing a crucifix during that time of my life, I may have remarked at least a few times, "Those crazy Catholics, they just have to leave Jesus up there on the Cross! Don't they know that He rose?"

Of course, Catholics do very much know He rose, but in Catholic theology, time is viewed a bit differently. Let me make up a little story to illustrate. A man is hiking on a summer day through a thickly forested valley and becomes thirsty, but he has no water. He comes across a fresh, clean stream and takes a drink from it, then goes on his way straight, while the stream takes a sharp bend away from him to the left. A half hour later, he gets thirsty again, but he comes across another stream, as fresh as the first, takes another drink from it, and goes on his way, again opposite the direction of the stream. A half hour later, the same thing happens, and he remarks to himself how extraordinary it is that all the streams in these parts have such clean, potable water. High on a mountain ridge-top above this valley, an old man is sitting on his cabin's front porch, watching the scene below and serenely puffing on his corncob pipe. From inside the cabin his wife calls out, "Gus, whatcha doin'?" Gus calls back, "There's a man down there who keeps a-stoppin' to take drinks outta Winding Creek." Gus could see that the man was drinking out of the same winding stream each time, drinking from essentially the same water source but at different locations along its bank. If the stream represents time, we humans see only a little of it at a time and do not know what is up ahead or which way it will turn, while our transcendent God, from "above", sees all of time at once, just as Gus sees all of the creek at once, that is, as "now". Time is all "now" to God.

We humans see the Crucifixion and the Resurrection as two events in the past, but God sees them both as equally and everlastingly "present". Both are crucial and eternal and stand side by side; one does not supersede the other. (The word *crucial*, in fact, comes from the Latin *crux*, for "cross".) And so, when Catholics celebrate the Holy Eucharist at Mass, they are not sacrificing Christ over and over again, as I used to think. Rather, they are dipping into the same water of life again and again from the one timeless "now" of the ever-present stream of Christ's Passion and Resurrection, which He gave to us physically and immanently in the sacrament.

Immanence and Transcendence in Music

Jesus wanted us to have an immanent experience of His continued presence in our physical bodies, because, in substance, we humans are not only spiritual beings but whole persons marked by the union of soul *and* body, and we have a need to know and worship and experience His real presence in the physical world. Just think: If a toddler's mother only told him she loved him but never touched or hugged him physically, he would suffer greatly from it. When John 6:48–58 (the "Bread of Life" discourse) is read in this light—and in the light of the contemporaneous documents and practices of the early Church—it testifies to Christ's supernatural presence in the Eucharist.

What does all of this have to do with music? We have seen that a piece of music consists of dynamic forms of molecular matter in the air, shaped and flowing through the stream of chronological time. We know that we outwardly, physically experience a piece of music as a soundwave event, perceived as a kind of statement through time. This is the immanence of music in the physical world, God's physical gift to us via our ears, which, by the way, are also a gift. And just as we in the Eucharist can step out of chronological time and partake of God's timeless realm, so too can we interiorly experience a work of music *as a whole*, transcending mere time and sound, as a powerful spiritual symbol. Yes, we do listen through time, one note at a time, in real time. But as the piece progresses, we also experience what psychologists call *cumulative disposition*. Let us use a passage of literature as an example, from chapter 15 of Charles Dickens' *David Copperfield*, where the narrator introduces us to the colorful character Uriah Heep, starting with his face:

> It was quite as cadaverous as it had looked in the window, though in the grain of it there was that tinge of red which is sometimes to be observed in the skins of red-haired people. It belonged to a red-haired person—a youth of fifteen, as I take it now, but looking much older—whose hair was cropped as close as the closest stubble; who had hardly any eyebrows, and no eyelashes, and eyes of a red-brown, so unsheltered and unshaded, that I remember wondering how he went to sleep. He was high-shouldered and bony; dressed in decent black, with a white wisp of a neckcloth; buttoned up to the throat; and had a long, lank, skeleton hand, which particularly attracted my attention, as he stood at the pony's head, rubbing his chin with it, and looking up at us in the chaise.[1]

As this passage unfolds through time like a piece of music, we gradually form a deep impression of Heep that is greater than the sum of its parts and particulars. Of necessity, he has been deconstructed (because one can name only one attribute at a time), but the magic happens as we reconstruct him as a full personality, as something more than a list of attributes. This applies not only to the passage as a whole but also to fragments. For example, "long, lank, skeleton hand" paints a far more vivid picture than simply "skeleton hand". The words *accumulate*; that is to say, each new word reflects back upon the previous words— "long ... lank ... skeleton ... hand"—to impart a kind of

---

[1] Charles Dickens, *David Copperfield* (New York: Penguin, 1994), 187.

transcendent feeling by the end, so that each word means far more than it would normally mean by itself.

After we have read the passage, indeed long after we have read the book, we carry with us, as if indelibly, this marvelous characterization of Uriah Heep and remember it fondly even after many years. But it is not the particular words that we carry, for we probably cannot quote them; rather, what leaves a lasting impression is the transcendent portrait and even personhood of the character himself. In much the same way, we are affected, even changed, by certain powerful passages or pieces of music. I have noticed, for example, a certain dreamy, almost reverent, expression come over people's faces at the mere mention of Debussy's "Clair de lune", because they bear a nostalgia for how it made them feel, for its cumulative transcendent effect as a whole, not just for its individual notes. The composition becomes all the more powerful when they hear it again later as an "old friend", because already from the beginning of the piece they have the entire message or spirit of the work within them. As with rereading a great book, they already know how it will turn out and so can enter even more deeply into the story as it unfolds.

And so I propose that this experience of music, indeed of much art and literature, reflects the Catholic theology of the Eucharist as being transcendent outside of time. It is a "re-presentation" and not only a "remembrance". We do not only remember Christ's Passion and Resurrection each time we receive the Eucharist, as a mere memorial, like visiting a grave. Rather, we dip our cup each time anew into the eternal, living stream of grace. It was Christ Himself who chose bread as the matter for this sacrament. If He had wanted us only to remember Him, he might have instructed us instead to view a picture of Him once a week. But bread differs from pictures: when we eat normal bread, we do not merely "remember" it each time we eat it. We are as freshly *nourished* by it as we were the very first time. So it is with the Bread of Life. Likewise, a piece of music being performed is not only a moment-by-moment experience in real time, re-created afresh in sound like bread right out of the oven; it also has a transcendent personality and identity outside of time that we can come to know *as a whole*, which can speak even more deeply to our spiritual souls.

In this distinction between the real-time experience of music as it plays and the transcendent, outside-of-time meaning of an entire work of music as a whole, we may have discovered a wonderful symbol of the Holy Trinity. The Trinity comprises lively internal relationships between its three Divine Persons, which the *Catechism* says are symbolized by the family (*CCC* 2205f.), with an internally dynamic, functional, syntactic, loving cooperation, each Divine Person doing a "common work according to his unique personal property" (*CCC* 258). This internal cooperation of the Trinity may also be reflected, of course imperfectly, by the internal coherence and cooperation, moment by moment, of such independent components as melody, harmony, and rhythm in a musical composition as it unfolds and operates in real time, each component also doing its work according to its unique properties toward a common goal. Overall, there is just one God who transcends time, and analogously, in any given piece of music there is just one overall composition that transcends time as a single whole.

If music can speak on these multiple levels *to* the spiritual soul of the listener, it can likewise speak deeply *from* the spiritual soul of the composer, if he has the interior disposition to make or engage this connection between the immanent and the transcendent. Exactly how can he do that? I must admit that, as a composer who has experienced this engagement, I am still at a loss to find entirely adequate words to explain how it works. However, I believe that if a composer at the professional level of his craft is, first and foremost, in a state of grace, prays for God's daily bread of blessing upon his work that day, and then simply "loses himself" in the narrative of his music (so that sometimes he thinks only fifteen minutes have passed but discovers it was actually an hour or two), he can possibly enjoy the engagement of his body and mind with his spiritual soul and at least have the potential to create music that speaks powerfully to the spiritual souls of others. Simply put, if an artist is inwardly disposed to grace and does his work "in the zone", as they say, then a transcendent, spiritual kind of creativity is more likely to happen. And if he is not so disposed and not in this "zone", some listeners may well discern that the work, however clever, sounds somehow disingenuous and contrived.

This is not a guaranteed formula, by any means, and it may sound far too mystical for some readers, but that is nonetheless the best explanation I can give. This spiritual engagement in the creative act is, I believe, something God does or chooses not to do with a willing vessel, just as it is God alone who "pours out" a performer, provided he is properly disposed and simply focused on giving a good performance. I do not mean to say that good, spiritually profound music will be "inspired" in the sense of Holy Scripture or even of private revelation, or to claim that it will necessarily be a masterpiece. The composer gives his work as an offering of worship to God and lets God do what He chooses to do with it in hearts. However God determines to use it or not to use it, the composer has been an obedient vessel, and that is his primary duty.

Catholic versus Evangelical Philosophies of Music in Worship

We come now to the physical and interior spiritual functions of liturgical music, and in particular, of chant—the ways chant and music generally are meant to function philosophically in the liturgy today. (I will save the *role* of chant for the next chapter—when and how chant and other music should be used, according to the teaching office of the Church.)

To set this discussion in a contemporary context, I will mention again that I was a Protestant who reverted to Catholicism in the early 2000s. Returning to Mass, I noticed many ways in which it appeared the Church had adopted Protestant models and modes of worship during my absence. One such change was, in some parishes, the complete absence of chant or of the Latin language. Pastors and bishops made this adjustment, I now believe, because they had been told mistakenly that Vatican II—or rather, "the spirit of Vatican II"—mandated such changes. However, these adaptations often had the unfortunate effect of watering down the Church's Catholic identity and obscuring many of the unique spiritual blessings and advantages offered by the Catholic tradition. I believe some Catholics also felt at the time that the Church needed an "update" to be more in line with modern culture and to keep poorly catechized Catholics from leaving and defecting to the more exciting social attractions of Protestantism. But adopting a Protestant theology of worship is not merely a cosmetic fix; it is a fundamental *theological change*, not an update.

Let us examine the Protestant philosophy of worship, indicating a few elements of it that many Catholic parishes have adopted. Evangelical Protestantism does preach about spiritual unity and a "church universal" as an entirely transcendent, invisible concept, but, lacking the *physical* unifying sacrament of the Real Presence of Christ in the Eucharist, it has sought to reflect that spiritual unity primarily through fellowship. During worship, unity is found above all in group prayer and group singing, but the phenomenon is most notable outside the liturgy. Protestant churches typically seek to unify or to reflect the unity of the body of Christ *socially*, from greeters at the door when you arrive, to Sunday school classes, to small Bible studies, men's breakfasts, and all kinds of other social events for all age groups. By comparison, most Catholic parishes have far fewer structured events and might even appear "cold" at first, to a Protestant visitor.

Why this difference? As a matter of philosophy, Catholics attend Mass first and foremost to receive and adore God in the Eucharist, as the Fatima angel taught the three children to pray: "Most Holy Trinity, I adore Thee! My God, My God, I love Thee in the Most Blessed Sacrament." Yet, though Catholics may not speak to one another very much before or after Mass, especially if they are in a contemplative mood and focused on communing personally with God, they do feel profoundly unified with each other in spirit as they physically partake of Christ Himself together as His body. Saint Cyril of Alexandria wrote of this unity in the Eucharist in the fifth century:

To merge us in unity with God and among ourselves, although we have each a distinct personality, the only Son devised a wonderful means: through only one body, his own, he sanctified the faithful in mystic communion, making them one body with him and among themselves. Within Christ no division can arise. All united to the single

Christ through his own body, all receiving him, the one and indivisible, into our own bodies, we are the members of this one body and he is thus, for us, the bond of unity.[2]

I have observed that in Catholic parishes where the Real Presence of Christ in the Eucharist is de-emphasized, the emphasis on Protestant-style social interactions by the parishioners during Mass and outside of Mass tends to be increased, and vice versa. (Likewise, in parishes where the congregation chatters loudly in the nave of the church before and after Mass in the presence of the tabernacle, the sign of peace goes on heartily and for a good while, often well into the Agnus Dei, when the faithful should be praying and preparing themselves to receive the Lord. In parishes where silence is preserved in the nave and talk is reserved for the narthex, the sign of peace, which is optional in the liturgy, is either eliminated or much more subdued.) Fortunately, in many cities, Catholic parishes are now springing up and overflowing with well-catechized young Catholic families eager to restore a truly Catholic philosophy of worship, while some of the older, more Protestantized parishes seem to be in decline.

At Mass, and before the tabernacle, we are together in the very presence of God. On the Mount of Transfiguration, the three disciples at first simply worshiped in awe, silently, side by side, spiritually unified; they did not need to hold a potluck supper! (I exaggerate for emphasis; I enjoy potluck suppers as much as anyone.) In Mark's account, Peter "did not know what to say, for they were exceedingly afraid" (9:6). Feeling awkward, though, he

---

[2] Cyril of Alexandria, *In Joannem* 11.11, quoted in *Catholicism: Christ and the Common Destiny of Man*, by Henri de Lubac (San Francisco: Ignatius Press, 1988).

eventually did suggest a kind of social gathering: "Let us make three booths, one for you and one for Moses and one for Elijah" (v. 5). But Jesus neither accepted nor even replied to this suggestion. Instead, "a cloud overshadowed them", and God the Father Himself came mysteriously into the foreground to speak to them about His Son (v. 7). Likewise, when we are in front of the Eucharist in Christ's holy presence, we remain silent and pray silently, but also we listen for whatever He might impress upon our hearts.

Alongside this most essential difference between Catholics and most Evangelicals regarding the centrality of interpersonal interactions runs a huge philosophical chasm in the role that music plays in worship. In Evangelical circles, one of music's main purposes is to unify the faithful, as well as to stir up a feeling of worship, which may take many forms: people singing vigorously together, for instance, or worshipers lifting hands and shouting "Amen" as praise bands raise the roof with moving—not to mention entertaining—song. Feelings of excitement and warmth connect the people together in fellowship and praise, appealing to their emotions. In the moment, this can feel profound and nurturing, especially for the lonely, but in my experience, such an emotional "high" can fade quickly by the next day, when the humdrum workweek returns. I recognize, of course, that there are some Protestant groups who do not place this much emphasis on emotional experience and who instead put the emphasis of their church service primarily on the sermon and Bible teaching. I am painting here only one type of scenario typical in some Evangelical groups and with some individuals, to make the point. Yet this point remains. There is of course nothing wrong with emotions, in their place, provided we do not let them rule us, or base our doctrine upon them instead of upon truth. If we are governed by feelings, we risk being "carried about with every wind of doctrine" (Eph 4:14).

By contrast, Catholic liturgical music in the Mass is *not* supposed to whip up the emotions. It is meant to be not only of little entertainment value but decidedly nonentertaining! Later we will see, too, how sacred music is, by definition, markedly different from the music we enjoy as entertainment, not a mere clone of it with Christian words substituted. As we will see in the next chapter, chant should have "pride of place" in Catholic worship. While supremely beautiful, it may well seem boring to those looking for an upbeat experience. No one I know is going to raise their hands in a Catholic church and shout "Amen" or applaud for the anonymous, blended, and impersonal voices providing ethereal chant from the back. That is because we do not go to Mass primarily to be pleased, any more than the people of Israel went to make sacrifices at the temple for their own enjoyment. The Mass exists primarily for God, not for us to have a good time. It is not all about us but all about Him.

Of course, we do also receive grace and blessing. Yet we do not go for the purpose of swaying and swooning with the flow of an emotional experience, though this a wonderful thing to do at a secular concert or a football game. That is not to say by any means that we cannot be emotionally moved at Mass. But in my experience, if a display of emotion becomes the yardstick of spirituality, some in the group can become "more emotional than thou", a subtler but equally wrong form of "holier than thou". It is possible for some of us to feel great emotion without displaying it openly, because worship is just as much, if not primarily, an act of the interior spiritual soul. Worship can also take place with great reserve, moderated by the virtue of temperance, or even in total silence. (To those who argue that we must provide teenagers with a kind of rock-concert, swaying-to-the-beat experience at Mass to please them and keep them coming, I will explain in the next chapter why the Church directs that those experiences, while perfectly fine for youth rallies, campfires, and meetings of all kinds, are not to be part of the Holy Sacrifice of the Mass itself. Teenagers, and even young children, can be taught this distinction and trained to spend one hour in reverence at Mass, which leaves them free to attend more lively concerts and events outside of the liturgy.)

In that spirit, the function of the serenely beautiful music of chant is to work in harmony with beautiful art, architecture, and statuary to create the holistic atmosphere of a sanctified sacred space. This requires music that, again, is *purposely different* from the music you would listen to as entertainment out in the world, that is conducive to a thoughtful disposition of interior reflection, penitence, and listening to God. When we walk into a Catholic church, we are, after all, entering a very unique kind of space, where the very presence of Holy God Almighty dwells in the Eucharist.[3]

In God's presence, Isaiah fell on his face, saying, "Woe is me! For I am lost; for I am a man of unclean lips, and I dwell in the midst of a people of unclean lips; for my eyes have seen the King, the LORD of hosts!" (Is 6:5). Likewise, Moses had to remove his sandals when encountering God in the burning bush (Ex 3:1–16). The fundamental difference between the Catholic and Protestant approaches to music in worship, then, has to do with whether the faithful are primarily in church to be in the presence of other people, or whether they are primarily there to be

---

[3] Vatican Council II, Constitution on the Sacred Liturgy *Sacrosanctum Concilium* (December 4, 1963), no. 112 (see appendix C).

in the Real Presence of God Himself, truly incarnate in the Holy Eucharist, regardless of who shows up. Protestants (and Catholics) do believe that God is present in the people, who constitute the body of Christ, because the Holy Spirit indwells them, both as a group (Rom 12:5) and as individuals (1 Cor 6:19). But they do not genuflect to the Holy Spirit in each other, while Catholics do physically genuflect and bow to Jesus as genuinely present in the tabernacle in that specific building. He also indwells Catholics, yes, but the Son of God is, in a special way, actually present in that particular, holy, set-apart place, surrounded by special architecture, incense smells, statuary, art, and special music, such as you will find in no other environment.

G. K. Chesterton said, "[The Catholic Church] is the only thing that frees a man from the degrading slavery of being a child of his age."[4] It is thus by design that the Church takes us back to liturgy and arts from the accumulated history of the whole Church age, supplying us with a concrete sense of the communion of the saints spanning every age, and of our own solidarity with them. It is as if we are worshiping alongside all our forefathers, praying and singing together with them many of the same prayers and hymns that they, too, used centuries ago—and that the Church has continued to use for centuries since. If you have ever walked the once blood-soaked beaches of Normandy or passed through the arches of the Roman Colosseum and begun, in that moment, to tear up, feeling the very weight of history in your bones, then you can understand something of the profound solidarity one might feel praying the liturgy with fellow believers from across

[4] G. K. Chesterton, "Why I Am a Catholic", in *Collected Works of G. K. Chesterton*, vol. 3 (San Francisco: Ignatius Press, 1990), 127.

the whole Church age, from the apostles to the millenni-
als. Missing out on this opportunity in the modern world,
many have succeeded in keeping up with the times but
failed to keep up with the timeless.

Protestants regard the church building not as "the
church" but only as a mere building in which the real
Church, the body of Christ (i.e., the people), meets
together—and were it not for the Eucharist, that would
indeed be a correct view. Catholics regard the church
building as sacred, a holy temple in which resides the true
presence of God in the Eucharist in the tabernacle. If only
one person showed up at a Protestant church service, the
presider would likely cancel the scheduled worship service, because it is, by definition, a corporate gathering. But
if only one person shows up at a Catholic Mass, the priest
can still celebrate a valid Mass, including the full liturgy. In
fact, though it is not ideal, a priest can even celebrate Mass
entirely alone; the re-presentation of Christ's Passion and
Resurrection will still take place.

What Makes Music Sacred or Secular?

Now we have laid the groundwork for defining the terms
sacred music and *secular music*. I remember having a hard
time with these terms as a Protestant. Back then, I wondered whether music should not simply be called "Christian" and "non-Christian" instead, with all songs having
Christian words categorized as Christian, whether played
in a church or on a car radio in traffic. I supposed the
more archaic word *sacred* could be used as a synonym for
"Christian", if someone preferred it. At the same time,
however, as a composer, I believed that I was writing my
string quartets for God's glory, which surely made them

"Christian" music, too, even though they had no words at all. After all, they were written by a Christian. In fact, from time to time fellow Protestants would ask, "Why don't you compose *Christian* music?" Usually they meant music in the contemporary Christian song genre, and sometimes, from their tone, I could tell that they believed I was not using my talents for God in secular classical music. In response, I would always explain that I am no good at writing pop songs and that I do regard my classical work as Christian. This did not sit well with one fellow in particular, so I asked him, "What do you do for a living?" When he replied that he was a housepainter, I said, "Why don't you only paint the houses of Christians?" He quickly changed the subject and then made his escape.

With an understanding of the Catholic Mass and of the church building as a sanctified, sacred space, the terms *sacred* and *secular* begin to make more sense with respect to music. *Sanctified*, according to *Webster's Third New International Dictionary*, means "set apart to sacred duty or use". That is to say, something sanctified is dedicated to a particular function. Thus, the special music used in that sacred space for Mass is itself set apart and sacred. It is necessarily different from music heard outside; otherwise it would not be set apart. Its original, principal use is in the sacred Mass. It does not ordinarily get played as car radio music, though it could perhaps be heard secondarily there. When you listen to Christian popular songs in the car—as some Catholics do—then yes, you are listening to "Christian" music but not technically to *sacred* music. Likewise, music for the concert hall may be dedicated to God, but this does not make it sacred in its function. In the same way, when incense is used at Mass it has a sacred function, while ordinary home incense (what I call hippie incense) does not have a sacred function.

If the church building is "just a building", without the Real Presence of Christ resident in the tabernacle, then there is no sacred space to set apart and so there can be no sacred music, only Christian music. Granted, the term *sacred music* is often used in the world—and by many Protestants—in a generic way to describe any music with a sung Christian text, as I myself had imagined. Even secular music professionals use *sacred* to refer to classical music with a Christian text, such as Handel's *Messiah* or Verdi's *Requiem* (which at ninety minutes for just the music alone is almost always performed in the concert hall rather than in an actual liturgical setting), or Brahms' *German Requiem* (which is for the concert hall and uses as its text not the Catholic liturgy but rather a collection of Scripture passages).

How can Catholic parishes whose musical attitudes have drifted from a sense of the sacred begin to reintroduce the true musical philosophy of the Catholic Church? I will address this in a practical way in the next chapter.

CHAPTER EIGHT

What the Vatican II Documents and Other Church Documents on Music Really Say

Let me begin this chapter by clarifying what it is *not* going to be about. It is not going to be about the Church's position on what kind of music we should listen to in our homes or in our cars or anywhere else outside of Mass, because the Church does not take a position on that, other than telling us to avoid intrinsic evil, which might in some cases apply to lyrics. I have faithful Catholic friends who play or listen to all kinds of music, from classical to rock, pop, jazz, country, Cajun, Irish, Broadway, folk, and beyond. This is a matter of individual prudential judgment, so this chapter should not be construed as taking a critical stance toward those genres of music. Instead, it will handle only the question of music at the Holy Mass.

Furthermore, this chapter is not going to be about my personal opinion about music at Mass. Rather, it will deal exclusively with what the Church actually, clearly teaches about liturgical music. Any of the styles just listed above might perfectly well be used at other parish events: fund-raisers, centenary parties for the parish, bingo nights, Catholic youth activities, fish fries, special concerts, cookouts, and so on.

Finally, this chapter is primarily intended neither to debate nor to defend the Church's documents concerning music and liturgy; its goal is only to present accurately what they say. It is not written for those who do not care whether they conform to ecclesial teaching, those who think they "know better", those who think they should decide for themselves what they want to do, or those who think they should be grassroots agents for changes to the timeless magisterial deposit of faith. It is written for those who wish to learn and to follow obediently the Church's literal directives. And to those who are shocked at what they learn here, I want to state that I do not wish to chastise anyone with these documents. My desire is simply to make known what may have been hidden from Catholics through no fault of their own.

With regard to Mass, Holy Mother Church has provided us with a number of documents that specify in detail how music should be employed, including *Musicam Sacram* and *Sacrosanctum Concilium*, which came out of the Second Vatican Council. These two documents (all of *Musicam Sacram* and relevant sections of *Sacrosanctum Concilium*) are included as appendices at the end of this book. There are also a number of important instructions for music in the *General Instruction of the Roman Missal* (*GIRM*), which can easily be found online. If our parishes and priests would revisit these documents, as we will do here, they might well conclude that many of our parishes have drifted far from both the spirit and the letter of these directives. Over the years, many have cited "the spirit of Vatican II" as a license to do a number of things in the liturgy specifically prohibited by Vatican II! As a starting place, I will cite *Sacrosanctum Concilium* on this general principle: "Therefore no other person, even if he be a priest, may add, remove, or change anything in the liturgy on his own authority."[1] If individuals can tinker with the Mass, it will not be long before we become essentially like Protestants in spirit, with individual parishes becoming quite different from one another as opposed to essentially *Catholic* (i.e., universal), unified in liturgy worldwide. (Yes, among churches, there may be small *regional* differences, but only as approved by the bishops.)

To achieve this crucial ecclesial unity, Catholics involved in the liturgy must familiarize themselves with and obey—not blatantly disregard—what the Church teaches in these documents, over and above their own personal tastes in music. I have learned in my life that people have very strong opinions about music, so I humbly ask the reader who disagrees with any points here not to "shoot the messenger", as my purpose is only to transmit the literal teachings as accurately as possible, quoting them and providing them at the end for the reader's own scrutiny.

Congregational Singing

All of our documents stress the importance of having all the people sing during Mass at certain times, where practical to implement. This chiefly pertains to "at least some parts of the Ordinary of the Mass *in Latin*" (italics mine).[2] However, it does not say *all* parts must be sung, whether in Latin or in the vernacular; in the section below on choir music, we will see that the choir may sing some parts of the Mass unaccompanied by the congregation, with the

[1] Vatican Council II, Constitution on the Sacred Liturgy *Sacrosanctum Concilium* (December 4, 1963), no. 22.3.

[2] Congregation for Divine Worship and the Discipline of the Sacraments, *General Instruction of the Roman Missal* (March 17, 2003), no. 41, para. 2 (hereafter cited as *GIRM*).

people *participating interiorly* instead. Indeed, even where these documents expound on the congregation's particular role, they make some possibly surprising statements about singing. One is that "Gregorian chant holds pride of place."[3] Yet in some parishes, there is no chant used at all! Of course, there may be some wiggle room in interpreting how much chant constitutes "pride of place", but surely "pride of place" does not mean no chant at all.

Is it really possible to integrate Gregorian chant into Eucharistic worship today? Some people who are partial to the songs and tunes they have been singing for decades may complain that (1) chant is too hard to sing, (2) chant is boring, and therefore, (3) visitors who attend Masses with chant might get turned off and not come back. To the first point, I respond that for the average person, chant is in fact technically and objectively much easier to sing than most popular styles, due to the narrower range of pitch and the diatonic (stepwise) motion of its melody. As a member of the congregation at many Masses where people with guitars were leading us in popular songs, I have observed again and again that very few people around me actually sing along. This is primarily because the rhythms are often syncopated and too tricky to keep up with, and the melodies rise too high in pitch and make too many unpredictable leaps, requiring vocal register shifts that many people simply cannot make. By comparison, in my home parish, which uses chant, the proportion of people actively singing is far higher! If the "spirit of Vatican II" is participation—that is, the number of people *actually singing*—chant wins, hands down. With regard to the second objection, that chant is boring, the previous chapter has already given a rebuttal: some people may *like* popular

---

[3] *GIRM*, no. 41, para. 1; *Sacrosanctum Concilium*, no. 116.

songs better, as entertainment, but our purpose at Mass is not to be entertained.

Regarding the objection (usually made by older folks) that visitors, especially young people, may be turned off and not return, I will first argue that this might have been the case with people who were young (as they were) in the 1960s and '70s, but nowadays, in my experience, it is just the opposite. Young visitors to parishes with traditional music are typically very moved and impressed by its beauty and are drawn to return precisely *because* it is so different. Have you noticed that traditional-music parishes tend to be overflowing with people in their twenties and thirties? Young people are probably repelled far less by chant than by a mediocre Catholic version of the same popular styles that Protestant groups typically do much better. (To quote one candid but possibly uncharitable young adult I know, Catholic church music too often amounts to "old, bald hippies with guitars playing elevator music".) Moreover, this objection of worrying about turning people off reflects a Protestant mindset. With no "altar calls" (beyond the invitation to receive Communion), the Catholic Mass is not primarily meant as a tool of evangelism. But even if to some extent it *is* such a resource, let it be the presence of Christ in the Eucharist and the beauty of the liturgy as a whole that draws them, not a few pop songs.

How, practically speaking, do we go about introducing chant into our parishes? The Vatican II documents specify that the people may need some coaching on how to sing chant (or anything else). Congregational singing must not simply be dumbed down, pandering to the lowest common denominator; it must be "intelligently fostered", and indeed the people must "know how to sing ... in Latin".[4]

---

[4] *GIRM*, no. 41, para. 2; *Sacrosanctum Concilium*, no. 118; Vatican Council II, Instruction on Music in the Liturgy *Musicam Sacram* (March 5, 1967), no. 18.

One way to encourage this, when introducing new melodies, is to have a little sing-through demonstration and rehearsal prior to Mass, just to familiarize people with the new music. I have observed this done in a few different parishes and find it very effective. The more common way is simply to use the same chant for many weeks in a row, and people will catch on and pick it up more and more each week, especially if a choir sings it loudly enough to "latch on to". Also, chant notation is relatively intuitive. Even if the people cannot technically read it, they can follow its melodic contour if it is provided on a handout in the pews. After all, the mysterious old notation of chant is simply a line graph, upon which you can see the notes move up and down (mostly stepwise) in pitch, and in just one quick lesson you can learn how to determine which notes are held longer in duration. A simple Internet search will yield any number of sites with simple instructions on reading chant, designed for nonmusicians. In my experience as a music educator, it is easier for the non-music-reader to learn than is modern music notation.

This next point may come as a shock to some. According to *GIRM*, neither the entrance procession, nor the Offertory, nor the Communion, nor the Concluding Rite requires music! Singing is an option for all these, but it might be done by the choir alone. In fact, the "closing hymn" is technically not even part of the official Mass rubric but simply a popular custom after the Mass has ended. Our Church's documents do promote outward participation in song on the part of the congregation, but this is primarily and sufficiently covered in the context of the actual liturgy—for example, the Kyrie ("Lord, have mercy"), the Sanctus ("Holy, holy, holy"), the Agnus Dei ("Lamb of God"). I am not saying it is bad to include songs during these parts of the Mass (provided they are approved songs), only that it is entirely optional.

GIRM gives four options for the entrance and the Communion: (1) the day's entrance antiphon or the Psalm from the Roman Gradual, sung by the choir alone or by the people, or else spoken without music, whether by the people, the priest, or a lector; (2) a seasonal antiphon or Psalm, with the same performance options as in number 1; (3) yet another approved Psalm or antiphon, with the same performance options as in number 1; and last, (4) a suitable, approved liturgical song (i.e., a hymn from an approved Catholic hymnal, not just any song).[5]

GIRM actually refers to these parts of the Mass as "the Entrance Chant" and "the Communion Chant", presupposing the "pride of place" (i.e., the best first choice) of Gregorian chant. What is more, *GIRM* lists the hymn option last, after the three variations on chant have been iterated. In some parishes, these official terms have been replaced by watered-down euphemisms. For example, rather than "entrance chant" or even "entrance processional", you hear, "Please turn to number four eighty-three for our *gathering song*." This seems to be part of a larger trend of softening our Catholic identity, such as when we call the narthex or the vestibule the "gathering space", or refer to the area of the church where the congregation sits as the "sanctuary" instead of the nave. (While Protestants call their whole meeting area the sanctuary, Catholics reserve that term for the area enclosing the altar and the tabernacle.) Another example of this phenomenon is naming the parish itself a "community", as in "Saint Stephen's Catholic Community", in line with the Protestant emphasis on community and social fellowship. Catholics instead emphasize Eucharistic unity, for only the *Church* of Jesus Christ, not some vague "community", has

[5] *GIRM*, nos. 48, 87.

been ordained by Christ Himself to administer the sacraments. Christ did not say to Peter, "Upon this rock I will
build my community."

With apologies, I will step on a few more toes by
observing that it seems futile for most Catholic parishes to
try to compete with Protestant houses of worship in the
performance of popular music anyway. Many big Evangelical churches nowadays have professional-caliber pop
singers and bands, theatrical stages with big sound, and
impressive projected backgrounds and light shows. Some
in my town have coffee bars and bowling lanes in their
buildings. One even does indoor fireworks on patriotic
days. If that is what someone is looking for, he will go
there. One could even argue that if we Catholics try to
do these things, and do them merely second-rate, this
might actually induce some Catholics to leave in search
of better and better performances. After all, this—along
with eloquence in preaching—is how some Evangelical
churches compete with each other for members and wind
up growing into "megachurches". However, it is also true
that the smaller and poorer "gospel" churches, especially
in the South, have their own rich tradition of old hymns,
truly talented gospel quartets, and congregational singing
in harmony that often raises the roof. When I came back
to Catholicism after many years in this gospel-church tradition, I was surprised to see that Catholic hymnals do not
supply all the vocal parts, only the melody! I had always
enjoyed singing the tenor or bass part on the hymns.

Yet Catholicism offers such far greater riches: the precious Real Presence of Christ in the Holy Eucharist; solidarity and communion with the saints through the use of
many of the same utterly beautiful liturgical prayers that
the saints themselves used; the worldwide communion
of the faithful, with many different gatherings of believers

from all over the planet unified wonderfully in the same liturgy. And the list could go on: Adoration, the rosary, many special prayers and saintly devotions, spiritual writings from centuries ago, and precious sacramentals. We do not need to mask our identity in order to pass as a second-rate version of the Protestants, musically or otherwise.

The Choir

Sacrosanctum Concilium specifies that as skill level permits, other forms of music besides chant, "especially polyphony, are by no means excluded".[6] This would necessarily indicate that some parts of the Mass may be sung by a well-rehearsed choir alone, since the congregation would not be able to participate in polyphony (music with many separate, independent lines going on simultaneously). Having the choir sometimes sing alone is perfectly in line with the statement in *Musicam Sacram* that the congregation's participation in the Mass is "*above all internal*, in the sense that by it the faithful join their mind to what they pronounce *or hear*, and cooperate with heavenly grace" (italics mine).[7] Having once been a Protestant choir director for six years, I applaud *Sacrosanctum Concilium* when it further says that the choir "must be trained to perform their function in a correct and orderly manner".[8] This entails an auditioning process, utilizing only qualified singers and not just accepting anyone who says he wants to sing. I have heard some choirs that sounded as if someone were strangling a cat. Directors need to be charitable but firm. According to

[6] *Sacrosanctum Concilium*, no. 116.
[7] *Musicam Sacram*, no. 15a.
[8] *Sacrosanctum Concilium*, no. 29.

Musicam Sacram, "Whenever, for a liturgical service which is to be celebrated in sung form, one can make a choice between various people, it is desirable that *those who are known to be more proficient in singing be given preference*" (italics mine).[9] This is not intended to hurt anyone's feelings but rather meant for the common good of all. Likewise, we would not want someone deficient in math counting the weekly collection. Each uses his gifts where they are appropriate. The same passage in *Musicam Sacram* goes on to say that if no suitable singers can be found, then it is better to let the priest either sing or speak the liturgy alone. It is desirable to have a choir but not mandatory. We should not try to force one together.

Even when a parish does have a good deal of raw talent, a certain discipline is required. Being trained—the criterion given by *Sacrosanctum Concilium*—entails, by definition, enough commitment and diligence to show up and sufficiently rehearse. But with this commitment comes a corresponding responsibility on the part of the choir director to account for the singers' limits, in both time and skill. In my experience, some ambitious choir directors bite off more than their choir can chew in their choice of music, with respect not only to the amount of rehearsal time they have at their disposal but to the choir's physical ability. In church, I often hear music that is pitched too high, causing the volunteer choristers to sound strained or out of tune. "The capacities of those who are to sing the music must be taken into account."[10] In defense of these directors, it is often difficult to find good music that is easy enough and pitched low enough for amateur singers. *Sacrosanctum Concilium* calls for trained composers to write high-quality

---

[9] *Musicam Sacram*, no. 8.
[10] Ibid., no. 9.

liturgical music that is accessible to the average volunteer adult choir, in terms of pitch and simplicity. I have so far created one such practical setting, with short-enough elements to be used in a typical Sunday Mass. It is sung regularly by typical volunteer adult choirs at two parishes in my town. It is reverent in tone and was easy for both to learn. So I do believe this call of Vatican II can in fact be heeded. Fortunately, today's software also allows an existing score to be transposed to a lower key; however, in some cases this alone will not necessarily resolve all the problems of ease and singability. Composers will still need to step in and compose music that has easier ranges, easier intervals, and simpler rhythms.

Finally, as it relates to the choir, I will turn again to the even touchier issue of the Catholic teaching that liturgical music is not a "performance". The documents of Vatican II and *GIRM* do not support—and in fact explicitly forbid—the idea that the choir or any musical group should be in the front giving a performance as "worship leaders" or as a "praise band". According to *GIRM*, the choir should not be in the sanctuary with the priest, where they can distract from the sacrament and seem to be on display. They should be "positioned ... as part of the community of the faithful" in the nave, which could mean in a side area, in the very back (the traditional spot), or in a choir loft, where they *face the altar with the people rather than facing the people as performers*. Their placement should not hinder them from worshiping as part of the congregation.[11] Although choirs should certainly rehearse and strive for excellence, this should not amount to a show-off "performance" but rather be an addition of beauty to the liturgical celebration.

[11] *GIRM*, no. 312.

It has been my frequent observation that people who once aspired to a career in popular music often find their way into church music ministries in hopes of having some outlet to perform. In light of this, here are three questions a director might ask prospective singers in order to discern their spiritual formation and intentions: Are you willing to sing in the back, relatively anonymously, rather than give what looks like a performance from the front? Are you willing to sing chant and blend in anonymously with a group rather than be a soloist during Mass, unless you are serving as a solo cantor? Are you willing to use only the approved musical instruments? According to *Sacrosanctum Concilium*, "No special honors are to be paid in the liturgy to any private persons or classes of persons, whether in the ceremonies *or by external display*" (italics mine).[12] This precludes not only the up-front placement of the singers but the inappropriate practice in some parishes of applauding after someone "performs" during Mass. Please do not clap at Mass. Just tell the singers how much you enjoyed it *after* Mass. If the director auditioning singers discerns that some people are wannabe recording artists looking for a performance venue, he should have the courage to explain these things to them. If it becomes clear that performing is their only real intention, perhaps he can direct them instead to musical events in the parish outside of the Mass, such as youth rallies or a parish coffeehouse, or simply invite them to sit in the pew as a faithful Catholic while pursuing their secular performance career elsewhere.

Sacred music should edify the singers and instrumentalists as much as the rest of the congregation. *Musicam Sacram* tells us:

---

[12] *Sacrosanctum Concilium*, no. 32.

> Besides musical formation, suitable liturgical and spiritual formation must also be given to the members of the choir, in such a way that the proper performance of their liturgical role ... will bring spiritual benefit to the choir-members themselves.
>
> In order that this technical and spiritual formation may more easily be obtained, the diocesan, national and international associations of sacred music should offer their services.[13]

The parish might thus support their music directors or musicians by having them attend a good church music conference, so that they are not only well rehearsed but spiritually mature and well catechized about the Catholic philosophy of music. It is my hope that this book might be helpful toward this end.

Musical Instruments Used for Mass

While it may come as a surprise to some, the documents of Vatican II do not support the use of any and all popular music instruments while the organ gathers dust. According to *Musicam Sacram*, just as chant has "pride of place", so "the pipe organ is to be held in high esteem". Instruments besides the organ may be used "provided that the instruments are suitable for sacred use, or can be adapted to it, that they are *in keeping with the dignity of the temple*, and truly contribute to the edification of the faithful" (italics mine).[14] This statement leaves space for a huge judgment call on the part of the faithful. Is a rock drum kit suitable for the dignity of the temple? Some may argue that it

---

[13] *Musicam Sacram*, nos. 24–25.
[14] Ibid., no. 62, quoting *Sacrosanctum Concilium*, no. 120.

depends on how it is used—that is, it "can be adapted to [sacred use]" by not playing it in too raucous a style. But if all instruments can be made suitable by using them in this way, what is the point of having this statement in *Musicam Sacram*? More telling is this statement in *Musicam Sacram*, number 63: "Those instruments which are, by common opinion and use, suitable for secular music only, are to be altogether prohibited from every liturgical celebration and from popular devotions." What instruments would those be? If a rock drum kit is allowed, if electric guitars are allowed, what instruments would be prohibited? It is hard to imagine instruments more exclusively "suitable for secular music" than those. What about a pop-band setup with microphones, drums, electric guitars, and Plexiglas sound baffles? Could such a rig be made suitable? And if chant has pride of place and the organ is held in high esteem, when will these instruments finally be used?

How, then, can we discern an instrument's place in the liturgy? Since the organ is to be the foundation of the instrumental ensemble, with other instruments considered supplemental, one might deduce that suitability also requires that the instruments brought in ought to sound compatible playing either along with the organ or just before or after the organ is heard. It might sound an odd mixture indeed to go back and forth in the same Mass between organ-accompanied chant and songs by a praise and worship band. Yet the organ ought not be the instrument we throw out of the mix. Some instruments that come to mind as compatible with the organ are the piano, solo violin or a string group, solo trumpet or a brass group, flute or other woodwinds, and the harp, though there could be others. If it feels odd to combine or juxtapose more contemporary instruments with the organ, then perhaps that is an indication of their unsuitability;

but the Church leaves this judgment call to the pastor or his bishop.

I have attended Mass at some parishes that do not even have an organ or that never use the organ they have. This clearly and objectively contradicts the statement in *Musicam Sacram* that the organ is "to be held in high esteem": not using it at all would surely amount to the lowest esteem. Notice, too, that *Musicam Sacram* calls it not just the organ but the "pipe organ". A true acoustic pipe organ, with air blown through tubular pipes that sound essentially like giant whistles, can be cost prohibitive for some parishes to purchase, in the neighborhood of a million U.S. dollars. The refurbishment of an older, existing organ might be more in reach financially for those parishes that have one in poor condition sitting unused. There is hope for those more modernized and economically limited parishes that still wish to implement Vatican II's musical directives. I would argue that to most ears, the best of today's electronic organs, some with faux pipes, can sound virtually identical to the real thing. Even the electronic keyboards used by most contemporary praise and worship groups have a variety of very good pipe organ sounds programmed into them, ready to be put into immediate use with the press of a button. Therefore, I see no legitimate practical obstacle to prevent a parish from implementing this directive of Vatican II.

We have seen that music at Mass is not supposed to be entertaining and should be decidedly different from the music of everyday life. It therefore stands to reason that we should not bring in instruments associated with the music of everyday life. We have also seen that the placement of the instruments should be with the congregation and not in front of it. But praise band setups are almost always in the front, where it looks like a very exciting concert is about take place. Musicians are used to seeing this kind of gear, but to the average person, and especially to teens, it is a very impressive, glamorous, and distracting sight, and it arguably gives the appearance of conferring "special honors ... by external display" to the people using it, even if they are truly humble and it is not their intention to do so. Although *Musicam Sacram* does not specifically prohibit any specific instruments by name, the Church does very specifically indicate the *placement* of these instruments. We have seen from Vatican II's own documents that the *real* Council is diametrically opposed to what is being done in some parishes in the name of Vatican II. We have seen that while some have accused more traditional parishes of being "pre–Vatican II", those parishes are often the very ones actually implementing the documents of the Council. Neither the spirit nor the letter of Vatican II was intended to give license to do anything anyone wants to do. Rather, those documents give us very specific instructions that we are to follow.

Vatican II in Practice

If a parish desires to reform its music program in line with the true teachings of Vatican II, how can this be done without confusing everyone and running off half the congregation? First, ideally, a true change of heart should precede or accompany any change of procedure. Some special parish retreats with outside guest speakers on music and worship, some basic catechesis about music worked into homilies (if it pertains to the Scripture readings), and some special articles in bulletins and on church websites may be employed, perhaps until the point is reached when a good number of parishioners are actually asking for reforms to be

THE SOUND OF BEAUTY

made. It is my hope that even sharing this book with fellow parishioners could get the ball rolling. Many parishes, perhaps some near you, have successfully reclaimed their Catholic musical identity, and they can provide resources and models for how reforms can be implemented. A parish could offer an additional traditional Mass, beautifully contemplative and reverent, at a special time on Sundays and especially enlist enthusiastic young people to be involved in its music. Or alternatively, it could offer a Vespers service with beautiful music and chant. These services tend to start with just a few people and then grow as the word spreads, until over the space of a few years a seed of beauty and reverence is planted in the hearts of the whole parish, and parishioners are ready to accept a phasing in of reforms over time.

However, it seems probable that the musical traditions of some parishes are so entrenched that they simply cannot be changed until the generation perpetuating them retires from the music apostolate due to age. In many cases, this may well take place within a decade. However, the question then becomes: What will the next generation do once the torch of parish leadership has been passed to them? At that point will come the moment of decision. Will they bring their parish's music into conformity with the documents of Vatican II, or will they go even further afield from the Church's direction? Younger parishioners hoping for reform would do well to anticipate and plan ahead in order to use this opportunity wisely and, especially, to hire the right people when paid music positions open. I now repeat an earlier statement in the form of a question: Is our goal as Catholics to "keep up with the times" or to keep up with the timeless?

In conclusion, I realize that this may have been a hard chapter to swallow for some readers, and perhaps it was a shock to learn what "the spirit of Vatican II" really was and is, especially if they have heard and experienced otherwise for many years. I invite the reader to read directly the Vatican II document *Musicam Sacram* and the section of *Sacrosanctum Concilium* on music, both of which are found at the end of this book as appendices and may also be found online at the Vatican website. Pray about it, and be open to new ideas, or rather to classic, timeless ideas, and to the teaching authority of our Church.

CHAPTER NINE

A Call to Leadership

Since coming back to the Church in the early 2000s, I have attended any number of Catholic conferences and talks on topics like evangelization through beauty, particular Catholic authors or painters, and general Catholic engagement with the culture. There, I have often heard a lament that the Church once had a leading role in the arts centuries ago and now is all but irrelevant, along with some general admonitions that we Catholics once again need to become a force for redeeming and renewing the arts. On a recent trip to Europe, I was deeply impressed firsthand by this truth, seeing several great cathedrals that displayed the leadership in superb art that once abounded in our faith. But seldom does the concern seem to go far beyond a pronouncement at a conference. What can actually be done?

Arts in the Church do not exist in a vacuum. The Church once had a massive impact on the arts in the secular culture, from the architecture of those unnamed masters who built the Cathedral of Notre Dame in Paris, to the statues and paintings of Michelangelo (*Pietà* or *The Last Judgment* at the Sistine Chapel), to the 105 Masses of composer Giovanni Pierluigi da Palestrina. These artists were not so much influenced by as they were *influencers of* the secular architecture, painting, and music of their day and beyond. One result was that ordinary laypeople, in turn, were more informed about—and present to—great art and music generally, and more artistically literate in their tastes and expectations, because they experienced great art firsthand in the Church. When the music of the secular culture gets dumbed down, laypeople will come into the Church with those same dumbed-down standards. But what can the Church now do to raise the standards of art in secular society?

A Five-Point Proposal for Artistic Renewal

Catholic University of America president John Garvey wrote recently about a chasm between the state of the arts in the world today and the ideal Catholic vision of the arts. He made the following statement: "I've been thinking lately about creating a Fine Arts Council at the university, whose charge would be not to appreciate this [secular, often purposely meaningless] representation of the world, but to rebel against it.... Perhaps if we can bring together enough people who see the world this way, they can inspire one another to a distinctively Catholic vision of the arts."[1] I myself had been thinking about something along these lines too. There are a few others as well, especially in New York and San Francisco, forming Catholic centers for arts and culture. There are a handful of very fine representational Catholic painters scattered about who might well come together with top Catholic musicians and other interested parties to work

---

[1] John Garvey, "The Empty Chaos of Today's Art Might Be Telling Us Something", *CatholicPhilly.com*, March 17, 2017, http://catholicphilly.com/2017/03/commentaries/the-empty-chaos-of-todays-art-might-be-telling-us-something/.

out a collective plan for some arts initiatives that would have some presence in the culture. Were this to take place on the national level, the institution might be called the "National Catholic Fine Arts Council". It could be an independent organization sponsored by private donors, by a faithful Catholic university, or even by a diocese or the United States Conference of Catholic Bishops (USCCB). Its primary job would *not* be to provide a place for Catholics to come and hear each other talk yet again about how the arts have declined and what we wish someone would do. Its primary mission would be *to do something*, or at least to facilitate things getting done. In this world, such action takes funding. Thus, a major goal of this council would be fundraising for specific artistic projects. Out there somewhere might be donors, both major and minor, whom God is calling to make this much-needed cultural renaissance possible.

As we have seen, there is currently something of a vacuum or gap in the arts, waiting, crying out to be filled by us. On the one hand, there are the fine arts, the contemporary examples of which generally have become so esoteric that the public cannot understand them and has little or no interest in them, as mainstream as they may portray themselves in their PR. On the other hand, we have the onslaught of popular culture, ranging from the very good and accessible (for instance, musical theater and some genres of music) to the very vulgar and awful. To fill the gap between these two extremes of high and pop culture, many educated people nourish themselves with the beautiful art and music of the past, which, fortunately, is readily available in museums, on recordings, and at concerts. However, I do not know how long such a situation is sustainable without *new* works of beauty, truth, and goodness being contributed to this treasury. Moreover, as

Pope John Paul II's *Letter to Artists* indicates, it is in fact the *duty* of living Catholic artists to make such contributions.[2]

I have in mind at least five projects a national Catholic fine arts council could undertake, some daunting, some easy.

1. **A large, beautiful building (whether new or purchased) to serve as a Catholic fine arts center, complete with a museum and a large and a small concert hall.** Such a center might have a permanent collection of great religious art of the past and feature temporary exhibitions of new paintings and sculpture (with or without religious subjects, but certainly beautiful) by faithful, living Catholic artists. It might have concerts of beautiful music of the past, performed by Catholic and other faithful classical music performers of all kinds, and host premieres of beautiful new works by faithful Catholic and other composers with a compatible desire for beauty. The technology to record this music professionally might be built in as well. The center might include a chapel where Mass could be offered; teaching and art studios where Catholic artists and composers could work in residence for a time; and conference space (perhaps in the concert halls) where relevant lectures and papers could be presented. It could have a theater for presentations of Catholic dramatic works, including (arguably) Shakespeare, along with lectures about them, not to mention a space for readings of great Catholic literature. Such a center would need to be visible, impressive in scale, and attractive to the public. In my dreams, it would be something like a Catholic version of the Kennedy Center in Washington or New York's Lincoln Center.

[2] See p. 73 above.

Such a national center would not preclude, but indeed might inspire, the creation of smaller regional centers for the arts dedicated to the mission of renewed excellence of craft and of attention to beauty, truth, and goodness in the arts.

The center would need to have a rather iron-clad mission statement and guidelines to protect its Catholic and artistic identity, lest it quickly become co-opted (even by some within the Church) and turned into just another secularized showcase for the same Modernism found in other places. The public could go there knowing they were going to see and hear something beautiful, and I believe they would indeed come. It would have to be carefully portrayed as a positive kind of "renaissance center", where wonderful things are happening, rather than as a negative kind of censorship center that emphasizes what they do not do. Most artistic venues today do employ subjective selectivity in what they include, sometimes with a biased exclusion of the traditional, truth be told.

2. A national Catholic arts commissioning program or arts competition with grants or monetary prizes to encourage the creation of beautiful new works of art and music. In such a competition, the winners' works would be shown or performed at the above-described center or some other prominent venue. The prize might also include the publication of a book of art prints or a commercially released recording of the commissioned music.

3. A national Catholic arts magazine, featuring art, news, artist profiles, and articles. Such a periodical might be issued annually, quarterly, or monthly as a newsletter. It could be in hard copy or online, depending on funding. Similar online sites are already springing up across

the world and might be happy to affiliate loosely with or be otherwise linked to this central site.

4. A national Catholic arts conference once every two years. This conference would be held at the center described above or at another large convention center, which would draw artists and musicians nationally for workshops and be open to the public for concerts, general lectures, and exhibitions.

5. A national Catholic arts council review and ratings committee, presenting the public with helpful reviews of films, music, theater, and art from a Catholic perspective. This committee could bring to the fore and promote little-known works by Catholic artists as well as comment upon those already known. It could send out press releases and other publicity about new works by faithful Catholic artists and musicians. Rather than award a censorship-style rating (e.g., NC-17, R, PG-13), it would award one to five stars for Catholic identity and themes, as well as for beauty and excellence of craft.

Now, you may say, the above five points sound good in theory, but from where will all these wonderful artists and composers come? Given that so many art and music schools are primarily teaching painters and composers Modernist techniques—or rather *not* teaching traditional ones—there rightly should be some concern as to whether there exist enough excellent traditional artists today to populate a Catholic arts center. I am sorry to say that I do not believe there are enough at this time. A few of us with a clear personal mission have overcome this deficit in the academy by training on our own. So perhaps the renaissance must begin precisely there: with education.

A Proposal for Artistic Renewal
in Catholic Higher Education

Traditional artistic education may likely be considered absolute phase 1, prior to—or at least concurrent with—any implementation of the five points I have proposed above. Creating an opportunity for traditional training ought to be paramount for any Catholic who believes and pronounces that we need a Catholic renewal of beauty in the arts. In the words of *Sacrosanctum Concilium*, "Composers, filled with the Christian spirit, should feel that their vocation is to cultivate sacred music and increase its store of treasures."[3] But how can they do that without training? Where are our faithful Catholic colleges in providing such training? Unfortunately, it appears that most of them, far from providing leadership in the arts in this culture, are MIA, or else—to use a cynical old expression—just rearranging the deck chairs on the *Titanic* of the world's increasingly marginalized and disregarded classical and sacred music culture. If we say we need a revival in these art forms, shouldn't at least some of our faithful Catholic colleges be offering them as a major?

Looking at the curricula of the faithful Catholic colleges listed by the Cardinal Newman Society, only about one-third have a music major. And these programs are largely devoted to maintenance of the status quo, that is, supplying organists and choir directors for parishes—though some are indeed spearheading a revival in traditional liturgy and chant. The only college on the Newman Society list that offers a music composition major appears to have a program much like other Catholic universities not listed by

---

[3] *Sacrosanctum Concilium*, no. 121.

the Newman Society, with faculty and students pursuing an essentially secular, Modernist aesthetic and curriculum.

If I may dream once again, how wonderful it would be if even one faithful Catholic college could create a music composition major or studio art major with a truly Catholic mission statement. Such a school would implement this mission first in the process of hiring faculty composers, actually listening to the music that the faculty applicants have composed instead of merely looking at their degrees. How many Catholic college administrators are even aware of what their own faculty composers and artists (if any) are doing, not to mention what they are teaching their students to do? Once an artist already on the faculty is entrenched in a completely non-Catholic aesthetic, it is tricky and perhaps even too late for the administration to challenge his academic freedom or to fire him, especially if he has tenure. But the school can at least hire new faculty who do have a Catholic philosophy, with work that demonstrates it.

Surveying these Newman colleges, I noticed that a few of them do offer majors in communications, media, film, and television production, which is promising. However, they have no music composition major to go hand in hand with them—strange, considering that most radio, television, and film works need accompanying music. Here is an opportunity to undertake the above mission of establishing a new major in coordination with a department already well established.

Some of the Newman colleges do offer degrees in music education, and I would challenge them, for their part, to teach their future Catholic school music instructors specific techniques for imparting Catholic formation through music (e.g., the music and virtue lessons in chapter 5), if they are not doing so already. There is the Ward Method, an innovative method of music instruction developed for Catholic elementary school children, but there is always room for more music education textbooks and sample lesson plans that strongly integrate faith lessons with arts training. Thus, there would seem to be a good opportunity now for faithful Catholics in the field of Catholic education to develop such materials. Otherwise, the students may be learning religion in one class (or "compartment") and music in another, without making the connection.

If I sound like a prophet in the wilderness in proposing all of these schemes in the realm of Catholic education, I can assure the reader that I understand it often all comes down to money. Making such dreams a reality requires a common passionate vision on the part of major donors and the people who will implement the plan. It requires at least enough capital to finance the necessary space, equipment, and faculty salaries until tuition revenues and scholarship funds make the programs viable on their own.

Influencing the Culture Using Contemporary Marketing Methods

I would like to propose some fresh thinking in regard to careers in music. The entire secular, commercial music industry has been in a huge transition since the early 2000s as the sales structures have moved from cassettes and CDs to the digital realm. The availability of self-marketing through social media is widespread and still developing, allowing essentially anyone with an Internet connection to create "indie" (independent) projects and sell thousands of streaming plays online without the support of a record company. I know of one innovative Catholic entrepreneur, Jimmy Mitchell, who has started a music production and distribution company called Love Good Culture for recording artists who wish to restore goodness, quality, and beauty to popular music culture. It is something like a co-op for independent artists, and he has a podcast and blog that reach a wide young audience—some Catholic, some not—to make these recordings known and to discuss pressing themes like fame, money, and the true meaning of beauty. In this new digital climate, there are good opportunities for Catholic artists to explore, and there could likewise be some great opportunities for Catholic universities. Two of the schools on the Newman list offer courses in the growing fields of arts management and music business. It would not be too hard for some other schools, following suit, to add at least a course or two in these subjects to their business curricula, encouraging Catholic managers to work hand in hand with Catholic artists.

Listening to Classical Music— for Beginners

In order for all of us to prepare ourselves for greater leadership in the arts, I believe we should enrich ourselves personally with increased exposure to great music. When speaking to groups, I often encounter people who tell me they would love to begin to add some classical music to their listening diets but do not know where to begin. Although it is beyond the scope of this book to provide such preparation in any comprehensive way, I have prepared in appendix A a list of musical compositions by twenty different composers (in some cases two or three works by the same composer, and in one case of shameless self-promotion, one piece by yours truly). These pieces are perfect for the "beginner", all with memorable melodies.

Start by finding them online as free videos and taking a listen, and then purchase a quality recording of your favorite works to listen to many times.

I wish you happy listening for enjoyment, intellectual refreshment, and spiritual nourishment. Try to resist multitasking. Listen attentively and deeply with your whole person and with the discernment of your spiritual soul, thanking God for His gifts of sound, hearing, and beauty.

APPENDIX A

A Beginner's Classical Music Playlist

Compositions are listed in alphabetical order by composer. Compositions marked with a dagger (†) are particularly user-friendly.

1. Beethoven, Ludwig van
   † Piano Sonata, op. 27, no. 2 (*Moonlight*) (for solo piano)
   Piano Concerto no. 4 (for solo piano with orchestra)
2. Borodin, Alexander
   † "Polovtsian Dances" from *Prince Igor* (for orchestra, with or without choir)
3. Brahms, Johannes
   Symphony no. 2 in D Major, op. 73 (for orchestra)
4. Chopin, Frédéric
   † Nocturne in E-flat Major, op. 9, no. 2 (for solo piano, or arranged for other instruments)
5. Debussy, Claude
   "Rêverie" (for solo piano)
   † "Clair de lune" (for solo piano)

6. Dvořák,* Antonín

Symphony no. 9 (*From the New World*) (for orchestra)

7. Elgar, Edward

"Nimrod" from *Enigma Variations* (for orchestra)

8. Fauré, Gabriel

Requiem, op. 48 (for choir with orchestra)

Élégie, op. 24 (for solo cello and orchestra)

9. Grieg, Edvard

† *Peer Gynt* Suites nos. 1 and 2 (for orchestra)

† "Notturno" from *Lyric Suite* (for orchestra)

10. Holst, Gustav

"Jupiter" from *The Planets* (for orchestra)

11. Kurek, Michael

Serenade for Violoncello and Harp (for cello and harp)

12. Lauridsen, Morten

"O magnum mysterium" (for a cappella choir)

13. Massenet, Jules

† "Méditation" from *Thaïs* (originally for solo violin with orchestra)

14. Puccini, Giacomo

† "O mio babbino caro" from *Gianni Schicchi* (for soprano with orchestra; opera)

15. Rachmaninoff, Sergei

Piano Concerto no. 2 in C minor (for solo piano with orchestra)

16. Ravel, Maurice

"Pavane pour une infante défunte" (for solo piano or orchestra)

Daphnis et Chloé, Suites 1 and 2 (for orchestra)

String Quartet in F Major

---

* *Dvořák* is pronounced "duh-VOR-zhock".

17. RIMSKY-KORSAKOV, NIKOLAI
    Scheherazade (for orchestra)
18. SAINT-SAËNS, CAMILLE
    Symphony no. 3 (*Organ Symphony*) (for orchestra)
19. TCHAIKOVSKY, PETER
    Suite from *Swan Lake* (for orchestra)
    Suite from *Sleeping Beauty* (for orchestra)
    Romeo and Juliet (for orchestra)
20. VAUGHAN WILLIAMS, RALPH
    † *Fantasia on Greensleeves* (for orchestra)
    The Lark Ascending (for orchestra)

Instruction on Music in the Liturgy *Musicam Sacram*

Second Vatican Council and Sacred Congregation
of Rites, March 5, 1967

Preface

1. Sacred music, in those aspects which concern the liturgical renewal, was carefully considered by the Second Vatican Ecumenical Council. It explained its role in divine services, issued a number of principles and laws on this subject in the Constitution on the Liturgy [*Sacrosanctum Concilium*], and devoted to it an entire chapter of the same Constitution.

2. The decisions of the Council have already begun to be put into effect in the recently undertaken liturgical renewal. But the new norms concerning the arrangement of the sacred rites and the active participation of the faithful have given rise to several problems regarding sacred music and its ministerial role. These problems appear to be able to be solved by expounding more fully certain relevant principles of the Constitution on the Liturgy.

3. Therefore the Consilium set up to implement the Constitution on the Liturgy, on the instructions of the Holy Father, has carefully considered these questions and

prepared the present Instruction. This does not, however, gather together all the legislation on sacred music; it only establishes the principal norms which seem to be more necessary for our own day. It is, as it were, a continuation and complement of the preceding Instruction of this Sacred Congregation, prepared by this same Consilium on 26 September 1964, for the correct implementation of the Liturgy Constitution.

4. It is to be hoped that pastors of souls, musicians and the faithful will gladly accept these norms and put them into practice, uniting their efforts to attain the true purpose of sacred music, "which is the glory of God and the sanctification of the faithful."[1]

  (a) By sacred music is understood that which, being created for the celebration of divine worship, is endowed with a certain holy sincerity of form.[2]

  (b) The following come under the title of sacred music here: Gregorian chant, sacred polyphony in its various forms both ancient and modern, sacred music for the organ and other approved instruments, and sacred popular music, be it liturgical or simply religious.[3]

I. Some General Norms

5. Liturgical worship is given a more noble form when it is celebrated in song, with the ministers of each degree fulfilling their ministry and the people participating in it.[4]

---

[1] Constitution on the Sacred Liturgy *Sacrosanctum Concilium* (December 4, 1963), no. 112.

[2] Cf. St. Pius X, motu proprio *Tra le sollecitudini* (November 22, 1903), no. 2.

[3] Cf. Instruction of the Sacred Congregation of Rites (September 3, 1958), no. 4.

[4] Cf. *Sacrosanctum Concilium*, no. 113.

Indeed, through this form, prayer is expressed in a more attractive way, the mystery of the liturgy, with its hierarchical and community nature, is more openly shown, the unity of hearts is more profoundly achieved by the union of voices, minds are more easily raised to heavenly things by the beauty of the sacred rites, and the whole celebration more clearly prefigures that heavenly liturgy which is enacted in the holy city of Jerusalem.

Pastors of souls will therefore do all they can to achieve this form of celebration.

They will try to work out how that assignment of different parts to be performed and duties to be fulfilled, which characterizes sung celebrations, may be transferred even to celebrations which are not sung, but at which the people are present. Above all one must take particular care that the necessary ministers are obtained and that these are suitable, and that the active participation of the people is encouraged.

The practical preparation for each liturgical celebration should be done in a spirit of cooperation by all parties concerned, under the guidance of the rector of the church, whether it be in ritual, pastoral or musical matters.

6. The proper arrangement of a liturgical celebration requires the due assignment and performance of certain functions, by which "each person, minister or layman, should carry out all and only those parts which pertain to his office by the nature of the rite and the norms of the liturgy."[5] This also demands that the meaning and proper nature of each part and of each song be carefully observed. To attain this, those parts especially should be sung which by their very nature require to be sung, using the kind and form of music which is proper to their character.

[5] Ibid., no. 28.

7. Between the solemn, fuller form of liturgical celebration, in which everything that demands singing is in fact sung, and the simplest form, in which singing is not used, there can be various degrees according to the greater or lesser place allotted to singing. However, in selecting the parts which are to be sung, one should start with those that are by their nature of greater importance, and especially those which are to be sung by the priest or by the ministers, with the people replying, or those which are to be sung by the priest and people together. The other parts may be gradually added according as they are proper to the people alone or to the choir alone.

8. Whenever, for a liturgical service which is to be celebrated in sung form, one can make a choice between various people, it is desirable that those who are known to be more proficient in singing be given preference; this is especially the case in more solemn liturgical celebrations and in those which either require more difficult singing, or are transmitted by radio or television.[6]

If, however, a choice of this kind cannot be made, and the priest or minister does not possess a voice suitable for the proper execution of the singing, he can render without singing one or more of the more difficult parts which concern him, reciting them in a loud and distinct voice. However, this must not be done merely for the convenience of the priest or minister.

9. In selecting the kind of sacred music to be used, whether it be for the choir or for the people, the capacities of those who are to sing the music must be taken into account. No kind of sacred music is prohibited from liturgical actions by the Church as long as it corresponds to the spirit of the

[6] Instruction of the Sacred Congregation of Rites, September 3, 1958, no. 95.

liturgical celebration itself and the nature of its individual parts,[7] and does not hinder the active participation of the people.[8]

10. In order that the faithful may actively participate more willingly and with greater benefit, it is fitting that the format of the celebration and the degree of participation in it should be varied as much as possible, according to the solemnity of the day and the nature of the congregation present.

11. It should be borne in mind that the true solemnity of liturgical worship depends less on a more ornate form of singing and a more magnificent ceremonial than on its worthy and religious celebration, which takes into account the integrity of the liturgical celebration itself, and the performance of each of its parts according to their own particular nature. To have a more ornate form of singing and a more magnificent ceremonial is at times desirable when there are the resources available to carry them out properly; on the other hand it would be contrary to the true solemnity of the liturgy if this were to lead to a part of the action being omitted, changed, or improperly performed.

12. It is for the Holy See alone to determine the more important general principles which are, as it were, the basis of sacred music, according to the norms handed down, but especially according to the Constitution on the Liturgy. Direction in this matter, within the limits laid down, also belongs to the competent territorial Episcopal Conferences

[7] Cf. *Sacrosanctum Concilium*, no. 116.
[8] Cf. ibid., no. 28.

of various kinds, which have been legitimately constituted, and to the individual bishop.⁹

13. Liturgical services are celebrations of the Church, that is, of the holy people, united under and directed by the bishop or priest.¹⁰ The priest and his ministers, because of the sacred order they have received, hold a special place in these celebrations, as do also—by reason of the ministry they perform—the servers, readers, commentators and those in the choir.¹¹

14. The priest, acting in the person of Christ, presides over the gathered assembly. Since the prayers which are said or sung by him aloud are proclaimed in the name of the entire holy people and of all present,¹² they should be devoutly listened to by all.

15. The faithful fulfill their liturgical role by making that full, conscious and active participation which is demanded by the nature of the liturgy itself and which is, by reason of baptism, the right and duty of the Christian people.¹³ This participation
   (a) Should be above all internal, in the sense that by it the faithful join their mind to what they pronounce or hear, and cooperate with heavenly grace,¹⁴
   (b) Must be, on the other hand, external also, that is, such as to show the internal participation by

⁹ Cf. ibid., no. 22.
¹⁰ Cf. ibid., nos. 26 and 41–32; Dogmatic Constitution on the Church *Lumen Gentium* (November 21, 1964), no. 28.
¹¹ Cf. *Sacrosanctum Concilium*, no. 29.
¹² Cf. ibid., no. 33.
¹³ Cf. ibid., no. 14.
¹⁴ Cf. ibid., no. 11.

gestures and bodily attitudes, by the acclamations, responses and singing.[15]

The faithful should also be taught to unite themselves interiorly to what the ministers or choir sing, so that by listening to them they may raise their minds to God.

16. One cannot find anything more religious and more joyful in sacred celebrations than a whole congregation expressing its faith and devotion in song. Therefore the active participation of the whole people, which is shown in singing, is to be carefully promoted as follows:

(a) It should first of all include acclamations, responses to the greetings of the priest and ministers and to the prayers of litany form, and also antiphons and psalms, refrains or repeated responses, hymns and canticles.[16]

(b) Through suitable instruction and practices, the people should be gradually led to a fuller—indeed, to a complete—participation in those parts of the singing which pertain to them.

(c) Some of the people's song, however, especially if the faithful have not yet been sufficiently instructed, or if musical settings for several voices are used, can be handed over to the choir alone, provided that the people are not excluded from those parts that concern them. But the usage of entrusting to the choir alone the entire singing of the whole Proper and of the whole Ordinary, to the complete exclusion of the people's participation in the singing, is to be deprecated.

[15] Cf. ibid., no. 30.
[16] Cf. ibid.

17. At the proper times, all should observe a reverent silence.[17] Through it the faithful are not only not considered as extraneous or dumb spectators at the liturgical service, but are associated more intimately in the mystery that is being celebrated, thanks to that interior disposition which derives from the word of God that they have heard, from the songs and prayers that have been uttered, and from spiritual union with the priest in the parts that he says or sings himself.

18. Among the faithful, special attention must be given to the instruction in sacred singing of members of lay religious societies, so that they may support and promote the participation of the people more effectively.[18] The formation of the whole people in singing should be seriously and patiently undertaken together with liturgical instruction, according to the age, status and way of life of the faithful and the degree of their religious culture; this should be done even from the first years of education in elementary schools.[19]

19. Because of the liturgical ministry it performs, the choir—or the Capella musica, or schola cantorum— deserves particular mention. Its role has become something of yet greater importance and weight by reason of the norms of the Council concerning the liturgical renewal. Its duty is, in effect, to ensure the proper performance of the parts which belong to it, according to the different kinds

[17] Cf. ibid.
[18] Cf. Instruction of the Sacred Congregation of Rites *Inter Oecumenici* (September 26, 1964), nos. 19 and 59.
[19] Cf. *Sacrosanctum Concilium*, no. 19; Instruction of the Sacred Congregation of Rites, September 3, 1958, nos. 106–8.

of music sung, and to encourage the active participation of
the faithful in the singing. Therefore:

(a) There should be choirs, or Capellae, or scholae
    cantorum, especially in cathedrals and other major
    churches, in seminaries and religious houses of stud-
    ies, and they should be carefully encouraged.

(b) It would also be desirable for similar choirs to be set
    up in smaller churches.

20. Large choirs (Capellae musicae) existing in basil-
icas, cathedrals, monasteries and other major churches,
which have in the course of centuries earned for themselves high renown by preserving and developing a musical heritage of inestimable value, should be retained for
sacred celebrations of a more elaborate kind, according
to their own traditional norms, recognized and approved
by the Ordinary.

However, the directors of these choirs and the rectors of
the churches should take care that the people always associate themselves with the singing by performing at least the
easier sections of those parts which belong to them.

21. Provision should be made for at least one or two properly trained singers, especially where there is no possibility
of setting up even a small choir. The singer will present
some simpler musical settings, with the people taking part,
and can lead and support the faithful as far as is needed.
The presence of such a singer is desirable even in churches
which have a choir, for those celebrations in which the
choir cannot take part but which may fittingly be performed with some solemnity and therefore with singing.

22. The choir can consist, according to the customs of
each country and other circumstances, of either men and

boys, or men [or] boys only, or men and women, or even, where there is a genuine case for it, of women only.

23. Taking into account the layout of each church, the choir should be placed in such a way:
  (a) That its nature should be clearly apparent—namely, that it is a part of the whole congregation, and that it fulfills a special role;
  (b) That it is easier for it to fulfill its liturgical function;[20]
  (c) That each of its members may be able to participate easily in the Mass, that is to say by sacramental participation.
Whenever the choir also includes women, it should be placed outside the sanctuary (presbyterium).

24. Besides musical formation, suitable liturgical and spiritual formation must also be given to the members of the choir, in such a way that the proper performance of their liturgical role will not only enhance the beauty of the celebration and be an excellent example for the faithful, but will bring spiritual benefit to the choir-members themselves.

25. In order that this technical and spiritual formation may more easily be obtained, the diocesan, national and international associations of sacred music should offer their services, especially those that have been approved and several times commended by the Holy See.

26. The priest, the sacred ministers and the servers, the reader and those in the choir, and also the commentator, should perform the parts assigned to them in a way which is comprehensible to the people, in order that the

---

[20] Cf. Sacred Congregation of Rites, *Inter Oecumenici*, no. 97.

responses of the people, when the rite requires it, may be made easy and spontaneous. It is desirable that the priest, and the ministers of every degree, should join their voices to the voice of the whole faithful in those parts which concern the people.[21]

27. For the celebration of the Eucharist with the people, especially on Sundays and feast days, a form of sung Mass (Missa in cantu) is to be preferred as much as possible, even several times on the same day.

28. The distinction between solemn, sung and read Mass, sanctioned by the Instruction of 1958 (n. 3), is retained, according to the traditional liturgical laws at present in force. However, for the sung Mass (Missa cantata), different degrees of participation are put forward here for reasons of pastoral usefulness, so that it may become easier to make the celebration of Mass more beautiful by singing, according to the capabilities of each congregation.

These degrees are so arranged that the first may be used even by itself, but the second and third, wholly or partially, may never be used without the first. In this way the faithful will be continually led towards an ever greater participation in the singing.

29. The following belong to the first degree:
   (a) In the entrance rites: the greeting of the priest together with the reply of the people; the prayer.
   (b) In the Liturgy of the Word: the acclamations at the Gospel.
   (c) In the Eucharistic Liturgy: the prayer over the offerings; the preface with its dialogue and the Sanctus;

---

[21] Cf. ibid., 48b.

the final doxology of the Canon, the Lord's prayer with its introduction and embolism; the Pax Domini; the prayer after the Communion; the formulas of dismissal.

30. The following belong to the second degree:
   (a) the Kyrie, Gloria and Agnus Dei;
   (b) the Creed;
   (c) the prayer of the faithful.

31. The following belong to the third degree:
   (a) the songs at the Entrance and Communion processions;
   (b) the songs after the Lesson or Epistle;
   (c) the Alleluia before the Gospel;
   (d) the song at the Offertory;
   (e) the readings of Sacred Scripture, unless it seems more suitable to proclaim them without singing.

32. The custom legitimately in use in certain places and widely confirmed by indults, of substituting other songs for the songs given in the Graduale for the Entrance, Offertory and Communion, can be retained according to the judgment of the competent territorial authority, as long as songs of this sort are in keeping with the parts of the Mass, with the feast or with the liturgical season. It is for the same territorial authority to approve the texts of these songs.

33. It is desirable that the assembly of the faithful should participate in the songs of the Proper as much as possible, especially through simple responses and other suitable settings.

The song after the lessons, be it in the form of gradual or responsorial psalm, has a special importance among the songs of the Proper. By its very nature, it forms part of the Liturgy of the Word. It should be performed with all seated and listening to it—and, what is more, participating in it as far as possible.

34. The songs which are called the "Ordinary of the Mass," if they are sung by musical settings written for several voices, may be performed by the choir according to the customary norms, either a capella or with instrumental accompaniment, as long as the people are not completely excluded from taking part in the singing.

In other cases, the parts of the Ordinary of the Mass can be divided between the choir and the people or even between two sections of the people themselves: one can alternate by verses, or one can follow other suitable divisions which divide the text into larger sections. In these cases, the following points are to be noted: it is preferable that the Creed, since it is a formula of profession of faith, should be sung by all, or in such a way as to permit a fitting participation by the faithful; it is preferable that the Sanctus, as the concluding acclamation of the Preface, should normally be sung by the whole congregation together with the priest; the Agnus Dei may be repeated as often as necessary, especially in concelebrations, where it accompanies the Fraction; it is desirable that the people should participate in this song, as least by the final invocation.

35. The Lord's Prayer is best performed by the people together with the priest.[22]

If it is sung in Latin, the melodies already legitimately existing should be used; if, however, it is sung in the

___

[22] Cf. ibid., no. 48g.

vernacular, the settings are to be approved by the competent territorial authority.

36. There is no reason why some of the Proper or Ordinary should not be sung in said Masses. Moreover, some other song can also, on occasions, be sung at the beginning, at the Offertory, at the Communion and at the end of Mass. It is not sufficient, however, that these songs be merely "Eucharistic"—they must be in keeping with the parts of the Mass, with the feast, or with the liturgical season.

II. The Singing of the Divine Office

37. The sung celebration of the Divine Office is the form which best accords with the nature of this prayer. It expresses its solemnity in a fuller way and expresses a deeper union of hearts in performing the praises of God. That is why, in accordance with the wish of the Constitution on the Liturgy,[23] this sung form is strongly recommended to those who celebrate the Office in choir or in common.

For it is desirable that at least some part of the Divine Office, especially the principal Hours, namely Lauds and Vespers, should be performed in sung form by these people, at least on Sundays and feast days.

Other clerics also, who live in common for the purpose of studies, or who meet for retreats or other purposes, will sanctify their meetings in a very fitting way if they celebrate some parts of the Divine Office in sung form.

38. When the Divine Office is to be celebrated in sung form, a principle of "progressive" solemnity can be used,

[23] Cf. *Sacrosanctum Concilium*, no. 99.

inasmuch as those parts which lend themselves more directly to a sung form, e.g. dialogues, hymns, verses and canticles, may be sung, and the rest recited. This does not change the rules at present in force for those obliged to choir, nor does it change particular indults.

39. One will invite the faithful, ensuring that they receive the requisite instruction, to celebrate in common on Sundays and feast days certain parts of the Divine Office, especially Vespers, or, according to the customs of the particular area and assembly, other Hours. In general, the faithful, particularly the more educated, should be led by suitable teaching, to understand the psalms in a Christian sense and use them in their own prayers, so that they may gradually acquire a stronger taste for the use of the public prayer of the Church.

40. The members of Institutes professing the evangelical virtues should be given special instruction of this type, so that they may draw from it more abundant riches for the development of their spiritual life. It is desirable also that they should participate more fully in the public prayer of the Church by performing the principal Hours of the Office in sung form, as far as possible.

41. In accordance with the norm of the Constitution on the Liturgy and the centuries-old tradition of the Latin rite, the Latin language is to be retained for clerics celebrating the Divine Office in choir.[24] Since however the same Liturgy Constitution[25] concedes the use of the vernacular in the Divine Office both by the faithful and by nuns and

[24] Cf. ibid., no. 101.1.
[25] Cf. ibid., no. 101.2, 3.

other members of Institutes professing the evangelical virtues, who are not clerics, due care should be taken that melodies are prepared which may be used in the singing of the Divine Office in the vernacular.

III. Sacred Music in the Celebration of the Sacraments and Sacramentals, in Special Functions of the Liturgical Year, in Celebrations of the Word of God, and in Popular Devotions

42. The Council laid down in principle that whenever a rite, in keeping with its character, allows a celebration in common with the attendance and active participation of the faithful, this is to be preferred to an individual and quasi-private celebration of the rite.[26] It follows logically from this that singing is of great importance since it more clearly demonstrates the "ecclesial" aspect of the celebration.

43. Certain celebrations of the Sacraments and Sacramentals, which have a special importance in the life of the whole parish community, such as confirmation, sacred ordinations, matrimony, the consecration of a church or altar funerals, etc., should be performed in sung form as far as possible, so that even the solemnity of the rite will contribute to its greater pastoral effectiveness. Nevertheless, the introduction into the celebration of anything which is merely secular, or which is hardly compatible with divine worship, under the guise of solemnity should be carefully avoided: this applies particularly to the celebration of marriages.

[26] Ibid., no. 27.

44. Similarly, celebrations which are singled out by the liturgy in the course of the liturgical year as being of special importance, may be solemnized by singing. In a very special way, the sacred rites of Holy Week should be given due solemnity, since these lead the faithful to the center of the liturgical year and of the liturgy itself through the celebration of the Paschal Mystery.

45. For the liturgy of the Sacraments and Sacramentals, and for other special celebrations of the liturgical year, suitable melodies should be provided, which can encourage a celebration in a more solemn form, even in the vernacular, depending on the capabilities of individual congregations and in accordance with the norms of the competent authority.

46. Sacred music is also very effective in fostering the devotion of the faithful in celebrations of the word of God, and in popular devotions.

In the celebrations of the word of God,[27] let the Liturgy of the Word in the Mass[28] be taken as a model. In all popular devotions the psalms will be especially useful, and also works of sacred music drawn from both the old and the more recent heritage of sacred music, popular religious songs, and the playing of the organ, or of other instruments characteristic of a particular people.

Moreover, in these same popular devotions, and especially in celebrations of the word of God, it is excellent to include as well some of those musical works which, although they no longer have a place in the liturgy, can nevertheless foster a religious spirit and encourage meditation on the sacred mystery.[29]

[27] Cf. Sacred Congregation of Rites, *Inter Oecumenici*, nos. 37–39.
[28] Cf. ibid., no. 37.
[29] Cf. below, no. 53.

IV. The Language to Be Used in Sung Liturgical Celebrations, and on Preserving the Heritage of Sacred Music

47. According to the Constitution on the Liturgy, "the use of the Latin language, with due respect to particular law, is to be preserved in the Latin rites."[30]

However, since "the use of the vernacular may frequently be of great advantage to the people"[31] "it is for the competent territorial ecclesiastical authority to decide whether, and to what extent, the vernacular language is to be used. Its decrees have to be approved, that is, confirmed by the Apostolic See."[32]

In observing these norms exactly, one will therefore employ that form of participation which best matches the capabilities of each congregation.

Pastors of souls should take care that besides the vernacular "the faithful may also be able to say or sing together in Latin those parts of the Ordinary of the Mass which pertain to them."[33]

48. Where the vernacular has been introduced into the celebration of Mass, the local Ordinaries will judge whether it may be opportune to preserve one or more Masses celebrated in Latin—especially sung Masses (Missae in cantu)—in certain churches, above all in large cities, where many come together with faithful of different languages.

49. As regards the use of Latin or the mother tongue in the sacred celebrations carried out in seminaries, the norms of the Sacred Congregation of Seminaries and Universities

[30] *Sacrosanctum Concilium*, no. 36.1.
[31] Ibid., no. 36.2.
[32] Ibid., no. 36.3.
[33] Ibid., no. 54; Sacred Congregation of Rites, *Inter Oecumenici*, no. 59.

concerning the liturgical formation of the students should be observed.

The members of Institutes professing the evangelical virtues should observe, in this matter, the norms contained in the Apostolic Letter *Sacrificium Laudis* of 15 August 1966 besides the Instruction on the language to be used by religious in celebrating the Divine Office and conventual or community Mass, given by this Sacred Congregation of Rites on 23 November 1965.

50. In sung liturgical services celebrated in Latin:

(a) Gregorian chant, as proper to the Roman liturgy, should be given pride of place, other things being equal.[34] Its melodies, contained in the "typical" editions, should be used, to the extent that this is possible.

(b) "It is also desirable that an edition be prepared containing simpler melodies, for use in smaller churches."[35]

(c) Other musical settings, written for one or more voices, be they taken from the traditional heritage or from new works, should be held in honor, encouraged and used as the occasion demands.[36]

51. Pastors of souls, having taken into consideration pastoral usefulness and the character of their own language, should see whether parts of the heritage of sacred music, written in previous centuries for Latin texts, could also be conveniently used, not only in liturgical celebrations in Latin but also in those performed in the vernacular. There

[34] Cf. *Sacrosanctum Concilium*, no. 116.
[35] Ibid., no. 117.
[36] Cf. ibid., no. 116.

is nothing to prevent different parts in one and the same celebration being sung in different languages.

52. In order to preserve the heritage of sacred music and genuinely promote the new forms of sacred singing, "great importance is to be attached to the teaching and practice of music in seminaries, in the novitiates and houses of study of religious of both sexes, and also in other Catholic institutes and schools," especially in those higher institutes intended specially for this.[37] Above all, the study and practice of Gregorian chant is to be promoted, because, with its special characteristics, it is a basis of great importance for the development of sacred music.

53. New works of sacred music should conform faithfully to the principles and norms set out above. In this way they will have "the qualities proper to genuine sacred music, being within the capacities not merely of large choirs but of smaller choirs, facilitating the participation of all the faithful."[38]

As regards the heritage that has been handed down those parts which correspond to the needs of the renewed liturgy should first be brought to light. Competent experts in this field must then carefully consider whether other parts can be adapted to the same needs. As for those pieces which do not correspond to the nature of the liturgy or cannot be harmonized with the pastoral celebration of the liturgy—they may be profitably transferred to popular devotions, especially to celebrations of the word of God.[39]

[37] Ibid., no. 115.
[38] Ibid., no. 121.
[39] Cf. above, no. 46.

V. Preparing Melodies for Vernacular Texts

54. In preparing popular versions of those parts which will be set to melodies, and especially of the Psalter, experts should take care that fidelity to the Latin text is suitably harmonized with applicability of the vernacular text to musical settings. The nature and laws of each language must be respected, and the features and special characteristics of each people must be taken into consideration: all this, together with the laws of sacred music, should be carefully considered by musicians in the preparation of the new melodies.

The competent territorial authority will therefore ensure that in the commission entrusted with the composition of versions for the people, there are experts in the subjects already mentioned as well as in Latin and the vernacular; from the outset of the work, they must combine their efforts.

55. It will be for the competent territorial authority to decide whether certain vernacular texts set to music which have been handed down from former times, can in fact be used, even though they may not conform in all details with the legitimately approved versions of the liturgical texts.

56. Among the melodies to be composed for the people's texts, those which belong to the priest and ministers are particularly important, whether they sing them alone, or whether they sing them together with the people, or whether they sing them in "dialogue" with the people. In composing these, musicians will consider whether the traditional melodies of the Latin liturgy, which are used for this purpose, can inspire the melody to be used for the same texts in the vernacular.

57. New melodies to be used by the priests and ministers must be approved by the competent territorial authority.[40]

58. Those Episcopal Conferences whom it may concern will ensure that for one and the same language, used in different regions, there will be a single translation. It is also desirable that as far as possible, there should be one or more common melodies for the parts which concern the priest and ministers, and for the responses and acclamations of the people, so that the common participation of those who use the same language may be encouraged.

59. Musicians will enter on this new work with the desire to continue that tradition which has furnished the Church, in her divine worship, with a truly abundant heritage. Let them examine the works of the past, their types and characteristics, but let them also pay careful attention to the new laws and requirements of the liturgy, so that "new forms may in some way grow organically from forms that already exist,"[41] and the new work will form a new part in the musical heritage of the Church, not unworthy of its past.

60. The new melodies for the vernacular texts certainly need to undergo a period of experimentation in order that they may attain a sufficient maturity and perfection. However, anything done in churches, even if only for experimental purposes, which is unbecoming to the holiness of the place, the dignity of the liturgy and the devotion of the faithful, must be avoided.

61. Adapting sacred music for those regions which possess a musical tradition of their own, especially mission

[40] Cf. Sacred Congregation of Rites, *Inter Oecumenici*, no. 42.
[41] *Sacrosanctum Concilium*, no. 23.

areas,[42] will require a very specialized preparation by the experts. It will be a question in fact of how to harmonize the sense of the sacred with the spirit, traditions and characteristic expressions proper to each of these peoples. Those who work in this field should have a sufficient knowledge both of the liturgy and musical tradition of the Church, and of the language, popular songs and other characteristic expressions of the people for whose benefit they are working.

VI. Sacred Instrumental Music

62. Musical instruments can be very useful in sacred celebrations, whether they accompany the singing or whether they are played as solo instruments.

"The pipe organ is to be held in high esteem in the Latin Church, since it is its traditional instrument, the sound of which can add a wonderful splendor to the Church's ceremonies and powerfully lift up men's minds to God and higher things.

"The use of other instruments may also be admitted in divine worship, given the decision and consent of the competent territorial authority, provided that the instruments are suitable for sacred use, or can be adapted to it, that they are in keeping with the dignity of the temple, and truly contribute to the edification of the faithful."[43]

63. In permitting and using musical instruments, the culture and traditions of individual peoples must be taken into account. However, those instruments which are, by common opinion and use, suitable for secular music only, are

[42] Cf. ibid., no. 119.

to be altogether prohibited from every liturgical celebration and from popular devotions.[44]

Any musical instrument permitted in divine worship should be used in such a way that it meets the needs of the liturgical celebration, and is in the interests both of the beauty of worship and the edification of the faithful.

64. The use of musical instruments to accompany the singing can act as a support to the voices, render participation easier, and achieve a deeper union in the assembly. However, their sound should not so overwhelm the voices that it is difficult to make out the text; and when some part is proclaimed aloud by the priest or a minister by virtue of his role, they should be silent.

65. In sung or said Masses, the organ, or other instrument legitimately admitted, can be used to accompany the singing of the choir and the people; it can also be played solo at the beginning before the priest reaches the altar, at the Offertory, at the Communion, and at the end of Mass. The same rule, with the necessary adaptations, can be applied to other sacred celebrations.

66. The playing of these same instruments as solos is not permitted in Advent, Lent, during the Sacred Triduum and in the Offices and Masses of the Dead.

67. It is highly desirable that organists and other musicians should not only possess the skill to play properly the instrument entrusted to them: they should also enter into

[43] Ibid., no. 120.
[44] Instruction of the Sacred Congregation of Rites, September 3, 1958, no. 70.

and be thoroughly aware of the spirit of the liturgy, so that even when playing ex tempore, they will enrich the sacred celebration according to the true nature of each of its parts, and encourage the participation of the faithful.[45]

VII. The Commissions Set Up for the Promotion of Sacred Music

68. The diocesan Commissions for sacred music are of most valuable assistance in promoting sacred music together with pastoral liturgical action in the diocese.

Therefore they should exist as far as possible in each diocese, and should unite their efforts with those of the liturgical Commission.

It will often be commendable for the two Commissions to be combined into one, and consist of persons who are expert in both subjects. In this way progress will be easier.

It is highly recommended that, where it appears to be more effective, several dioceses of the same region should set up a single Commission, which will establish a common plan of action and gather together their forces more fruitfully.

69. The Liturgical Commission, to be set up by the Episcopal Conference as judged opportune,[46] should also be responsible for sacred music; it should therefore also consist of experts in this field. It is useful, however, for such a Commission to confer not only with the diocesan Commissions, but also with other societies which may be involved in musical matters in the same region. This also

---

[45] Cf. above, no. 24.
[46] Cf. *Sacrosanctum Concilium*, no. 44.

applies to the pastoral liturgical Institute mentioned in art. 44 of the Constitution.

In the audience granted on 9 February, 1967 to His Eminence Arcadio M. Cardinal Larraona, Prefect of the Sacred Congregation of Rites, His Holiness Pope Paul VI approved and confirmed the present Instruction by his authority, ordered it to be published and at the same time established that it should come into force on Pentecost Sunday 14 May, 1967.

APPENDIX C

Constitution on the Sacred Liturgy *Sacrosanctum Concilium* (Excerpt)

Second Vatican Council, December 4, 1963

Chapter VI: Sacred Music

112. The musical tradition of the universal Church is a treasure of inestimable value, greater even than that of any other art. The main reason for this pre-eminence is that, as sacred song united to the words, it forms a necessary or integral part of the solemn liturgy.

Holy Scripture, indeed, has bestowed praise upon sacred song (cf. Eph 5:19; Col 3:16), and the same may be said of the fathers of the Church and of the Roman pontiffs who in recent times, led by St. Pius X, have explained more precisely the ministerial function supplied by sacred music in the service of the Lord.

Therefore sacred music is to be considered the more holy in proportion as it is more closely connected with the liturgical action, whether it adds delight to prayer, fosters unity of minds, or confers greater solemnity upon the sacred rites. But the Church approves of all forms of true art having the needed qualities, and admits them into divine worship.

Accordingly, the sacred Council, keeping to the norms and precepts of ecclesiastical tradition and discipline, and having regard to the purpose of sacred music, which is the glory of God and the sanctification of the faithful, decrees as follows.

113. Liturgical worship is given a more noble form when the divine offices are celebrated solemnly in song, with the assistance of sacred ministers and the active participation of the people.

As regards the language to be used, the provisions of Art. 36 are to be observed; for the Mass, Art. 54; for the sacraments, Art. 63; for the divine office, Art. 101.

114. The treasure of sacred music is to be preserved and fostered with great care. Choirs must be diligently promoted, especially in cathedral churches; but bishops and other pastors of souls must be at pains to ensure that, whenever the sacred action is to be celebrated with song, the whole body of the faithful may be able to contribute that active participation which is rightly theirs, as laid down in Art. 28 and 30.

115. Great importance is to be attached to the teaching and practice of music in seminaries, in the novitiates and houses of study of religious of both sexes, and also in other Catholic institutions and schools. To impart this instruction, teachers are to be carefully trained and put in charge of the teaching of sacred music.

It is desirable also to found higher institutes of sacred music whenever this can be done. Composers and singers, especially boys, must also be given a genuine liturgical training.

116. The Church acknowledges Gregorian chant as especially suited to the Roman liturgy: therefore, other things being equal, it should be given pride of place in liturgical services.

But other kinds of sacred music, especially polyphony, are by no means excluded from liturgical celebrations, so long as they accord with the spirit of the liturgical action, as laid down in Art. 30.

117. The typical edition of the books of Gregorian chant is to be completed; and a more critical edition is to be prepared of those books already published since the restoration by St. Pius X.

It is desirable also that an edition be prepared containing simpler melodies, for use in small churches.

118. Religious singing by the people is to be intelligently fostered so that in devotions and sacred exercises, as also during liturgical services, the voices of the faithful may ring out according to the norms and requirements of the rubrics.

119. In certain parts of the world, especially mission lands, there are peoples who have their own musical traditions, and these play a great part in their religious and social life. For this reason due importance is to be attached to their music, and a suitable place is to be given to it, not only in forming their attitude toward religion, but also in adapting worship to their native genius, as indicated in Art. 39 and 40.

Therefore, when missionaries are being given training in music, every effort should be made to see that they become competent in promoting the traditional music of these peoples, both in schools and in sacred services, as far as may be practicable.

120. In the Latin Church the pipe organ is to be held in high esteem, for it is the traditional musical instrument which adds a wonderful splendor to the Church's ceremonies and powerfully lifts up man's mind to God and to higher things.

But other instruments also may be admitted for use in divine worship, with the knowledge and consent of the competent territorial authority, as laid down in Art. 22, 52, 37, and 40. This may be done, however, only on condition that the instruments are suitable, or can be made suitable, for sacred use, accord with the dignity of the temple, and truly contribute to the edification of the faithful.

121. Composers, filled with the Christian spirit, should feel that their vocation is to cultivate sacred music and increase its store of treasures.

Let them produce compositions which have the qualities proper to genuine sacred music, not confining themselves to works which can be sung only by large choirs, but providing also for the needs of small choirs and for the active participation of the entire assembly of the faithful.

The texts intended to be sung must always be in conformity with Catholic doctrine; indeed they should be drawn chiefly from holy scripture and from liturgical sources.

APPENDIX D

PRESENTATION ON MUSIC AND THE VIRTUES (FOR CHILDREN)

FORTITUDE

Fortitude means being like a fort, taking a stand.
It means never giving up when the going gets tough and
you feel like quitting.

How to Show Fortitude in Music

- Practice an instrument until it finally sounds good.
- Stick with choir or band during those times it feels
  more like work than like fun.
- Try again and again when you feel frustrated.

Some Results of Fortitude

- Satisfaction that you have finally learned to do it well!
- Satisfaction: You hung in there! Yay! Your performance was excellent!
- Humility, because you know it was God who gave
  you the ability and courage to do it.
- Gratitude: "Thanks, God!"
- Being a blessing to God and others—for example,
  when you sing or play to God at Mass or when you

learn to perform for people in a nursing home and bring them joy.

JUSTICE

Justice is the determination to give *everyone* his rightful due.

It does not matter what we think of a particular person.

"Fair" is determined not by what you want but by what you *deserve.*

Justice is a virtue of the will. You decide to do it, and you do it.

How to Show Justice in Music

- Play instruments! If you are following the rules and participating in class, you earn the time to play an instrument (boomwhackers, xylophones, hand chimes, and more). If you are not following the rules, you do not earn the time to play an instrument.
- Be quiet while each actor is rehearsing for the school musical, and support each other. Example: When Peter Pan asks the audience, "Do you believe in fairies?" and a student says loudly, "No!", is that a just thing for him to do?

Some Results of Justice

- You can rest in the knowledge that you will receive all that you earn, and only as much.
- You know that this principle works the same for every single person, not just you. Favoritism is out.
- You will be able to discern unjust actions and stand up for those who are being treated unfairly.

PRUDENCE

Prudence means to judge correctly what is right or wrong in any situation.
Prudence is a virtue of the intellect.

How to Show Prudence in Music

- Choose appropriate songs to listen to.
- Avoid listening to songs that are inappropriate, even if they sound good.

Some Results of Prudence

- You will be able to discern for yourself what is right or wrong in music.
- You will not need an adult to tell you which songs are good or bad.
- You will grow wiser.

TEMPERANCE

Temperance is restraint of our desires and passions.
Temperance keeps us from excess.

How to Show Temperance in Music

- Discipline yourself to practice and to perform.
- Do not throw a tantrum if you play something incorrectly or have to practice many times.
- Pay attention to the task at hand.
- Do not talk during rehearsal.

Some Results of Temperance

- You will develop patience and perseverance.
- You will be stronger in resisting temptations.

FAITH AND HOPE

FAITH

Faith is belief in God and all He has said and revealed to us.
Faith can also be belief in the presence of goodness in
others.

HOPE

Hope is the desire for the kingdom of heaven and eternal
life.
We rely not on our own strength but on the help of the
Holy Spirit.
We do not let ourselves get discouraged.

How to Show Faith and Hope in Music

- Play beautiful and excellent music.
- Remember that the reason for music is the glory and
  worship of God.
- Try to set the words of a Psalm to a chant mode.
- Pray the prayer to Saint Cecilia before music class and
  before practicing.

Some Results of Faith and Hope

- You will see things in life with a deeper perspective
  (like Superman with X-ray vision).
- You will have strength to keep running the race, as
  Saint Paul says, whatever happens.
- You will not give up on music because of a bad per-
  formance or an embarrassing moment.

CHARITY

Charity is love for God and others.
Charity is consideration for the good of others.

How to Show Charity in Music

- Treat fellow students and teachers with respect and kindness.
- Encourage other musicians when they are discouraged about their music.
- Help others—for example, set up chairs and music stands for rehearsal.
- Let someone else play an instrument before you do, when taking turns.
- Do what teachers and other adults ask you to do without complaining.
- Offer up to God and His glory everything you do in music class (singing, writing music, playing instruments, homework).

Some Results of Charity

- You will allow God to live more fully in you, since God is love.
- You will be closer to God and please Him.
- You will be more at peace, and music will be more fun.

APPENDIX E

VIRTUE RATINGS SYSTEM FOR SONGS: AN EXERCISE FOR YOUNG STUDENTS

Students can use a worksheet (fig. 9) to "rate" the level of virtue in songs. First, the students try the exercise in class together, each student working with a partner. The teacher plays a song over speakers and hands out the rating chart and a copy of the song's lyrics to each child. They discuss the song as a group and together determine its score. In explaining the exercise, the teacher should note that even though a song may not technically be "bad" (i.e., crude or inappropriate), it may still represent "empty calories", a kind of musical junk food. A little junk food may be okay, but overall we should strive to feed our souls with good musical "nutrition". Afterward, each student takes a blank worksheet home and rates a song he has been listening to lately. Students present their findings to the class within the next few class meetings.

VIRTUE RATING FOR SONGS

Using the following chart, "rate" the amount of virtue in the lyrics of songs you listen to. Look for the good in the song, but recognize if goodness cannot be found.

INSTRUCTIONS: (1) Score the song's lyrics on a scale of 0 to 5 according to each virtue. Zero means the song does not contain this virtue at all. A score of 1 to 5 means that it shows some virtue, 5 being the highest amount of virtue possible. (2) If you give the song a rating higher than 0 for a certain virtue, describe why. (3) At the end, add all the scores together to find the song's total virtue rating. (4) Use the scoring legend at the bottom to interpret your song's rating.

NOTE: If the song contains inappropriate material, it should be disqualified to begin with.

Song title: "Trouble When You Walked In"   **Artist:** Taylor Swift

Virtue	Score	Description of Virtue in Song
Fortitude	0	
Justice	0	
Prudence	3	She learned the hard way how to discern what's good.
Temperance	3	She is learning to moderate her emotions.
Faith	0	
Hope	0	
Charity	3	She's learning true vs. false love and possibly feels compassion for the boy.

TOTAL   9

Scoring Legend

Total Score	Meaning
0–5	Little or no virtue message; musical "junk food"
6–10	Some virtue message; may or may not be worth time/money
11–20	More virtue message; more likely to be worthwhile
21–35	Contains virtue; should be worthwhile (but see NOTE above)

Figure 9: "Virtue Rating for Songs" worksheet for young students, with sample responses.

APPENDIX F

Symphony no. 2: *Tales from the Realm of Faerie*[*]

Part I

I have lately had an idea that perhaps a classical composer could create a musical counterpart to the allegories of J. R. R. Tolkien and C. S. Lewis in the form of a purely musical "fairy tale in sound" containing hidden Christian symbolism. Clearly, this needs some explanation. First, I am not talking about embedding some secret spiritual code within a musical work to be discovered, as a kind of superficial game. For example, I am not talking about numerically transforming a biblical name into a musical theme or hiding a hymn tune written backward in the clarinet line. For the authors mentioned above, the Christian content was not a game or code but the foundation and genesis of the work's central conception. It generates the shape and architecture of the story and is its reason for existing. To illustrate how this might work in music, I am going to discuss a single musical example: the introduction (the first

* This article originally appeared in two installments in the Augustine Institute's online journal *Faith and Culture* on November 8, 2018 (pt. 1), and March 28, 2019 (pt. 2), with a few alterations. Excerpts from Michael Kurek's Symphony no. 2 can be heard on his official website at https://michaelkurek.com/bonus-video-a-work-in-progress/.

thirty-seven measures, about the first minute and a half) of the first movement of my second symphony.

This passage of music, along with the rest of the symphony, sounds to most ears like some kind of a fairy tale in sound. That is to say, with its Romantic orchestration and shimmering opening that builds up to a swashbuckling climax, one might suppose that it had been written for a ballet like *Sleeping Beauty* or *Romeo and Juliet*. As far as the public knows, though, I have avoided pegging this music to any particular story. In my program note, I have said only that it "calls to my mind the flavors of many fairy-tale worlds I have loved"; that way the listener remains free to imagine all sorts of things. However, for me there actually was a bit of Christian symbolism that literally inspired this excerpt, which I am about to reveal. I hasten to add that I do not plan to reveal any further Christian symbolism behind the rest of the symphony, even to Christians, for reasons I will explain below.

However, to make my point I will reveal that this musical introduction was conceived and inspired in response to one of the most spectacular events in the Bible, the Ascension of Christ into heaven, described in Acts 1. The Ascension, though awe inspiring, may have been a rather silent and hushed moment from the perspective of the apostles who were on earth watching it. Yet I cannot help but imagine the sound that the hosts of angels and saints in heaven might have been hearing, inaudible to earthly ears, which might have been quite ravishing. I picture throngs of Old Testament saints in something like a heavenly stadium, watching the Ascension projected like live TV coverage on the clouds—a very contemporary kind of image, but nevertheless, I imagine that they were enabled to see this event somehow and found it thrilling. This is purely a heavenly speculation, of course.

Perhaps, in *their* perception, moments before the actual Ascension, the air was supercharged by electrifying particles, like sparkling, magical dust. Then, with a rising horn line, as our Lord was taken up, they might have sent up great cheers, heralded by glorious chords and heroic fanfares from all the great trumpet sections of angels in raucous celebration. This would be followed by a trailing off, like sparks floating down after fireworks that have just exploded. And yet, since this would have been no mere welcome-back-to-heaven party, the tone of this music might also have been utterly serious and majestic, reflecting an awesome power and wonder and a certain kind of godly fear on the part of all who witnessed it. Now you can hear how very specifically the music of this introduction fits this description.

To the public listeners of the music, though, I will say nothing of this in the program note and mention it only here, and only with regard to this one short excerpt. It is enough for the public that they perceive something generally like an engaging and beautiful epic style. They might even suggest to their friends all sorts of stories or films with which they imagine it might go well. However, I am concerned only that they perceive a sense of some kind of musical fairy tale. Christ illustrated truths in archetypal parables, that is, in fictional stories about typical situations, possibly because such narratives transcend a particular time and place, a quality derived precisely from their being fictional. Although Christ's parables were about situations that could have happened in real life (but did not), and fairy tales are about situations that could not happen in real life, both can be seen as a powerful, more transcendent kind of fictional narrative that speaks of our ultimate purpose, our fantastic journey toward redemption and heaven. While a factual, nonfictional story may also exhibit such symbolism,

I believe (along with Tolkien, Lewis, George MacDonald, and others) that the more abstract fairy-tale genre in literature, like Christ's parables, may actually speak more deeply, naturally, and universally than a factual story can. By extension, as a composer, I believe that a musical fairy tale can speak with the same abstraction as a literary fairy tale—if not even more powerfully, due to the directly emotional potential of music.

It should follow, therefore, that it is not important for me to describe the rest of this symphony, blow by blow, in terms of specific Christian events like the Ascension of Christ, even if they were what generated the work. In fact, it is better that I leave this as a mystery, even if you might at some point think you are hearing the siege of Jericho or the dance of Salome. What is important is simply to know that this was my working method and that my work was, at its heart, the product of a Christian imagination. My desire is not that the listener perceive a certain event but that he discern the general spiritual values of goodness, truth, and beauty, and also an epic, compassionate, and heroic journey of some kind, in whatever way each listener may be able to imagine them. This is the mystery and the wonder of the sanctified human imagination, be it in fairy tales or traditional classical music. Unlike, say, Narnia, with its specific allegory of Christ's redemptive work, purely instrumental music can be an allegorical narrative more generally—of purposefulness moving through time toward a goal; of love, sadness, struggle, hope, and ultimate victory.

Part II

On November 8, 2018, in *Faith and Culture*, I proposed the idea of composing a musical counterpart to the great

Christian fairy-tale tradition of MacDonald, Tolkien, and Lewis. I explained how I intended the first movement of my Symphony no. 2, *Tales from the Realm of Faerie*, to be regarded in some kind of analogous way to those works of literature.

Upon completion of the second movement, I would now like to go a bit deeper into the comparison between instrumental music and the fairy tale, this time invoking George MacDonald's short essay "The Fantastic Imagination".[1] MacDonald makes several references to music, notably this one: "The true fairytale is, to my mind, very like the sonata." I will return to that particular comparison in due course. But first it would be good to make a certain distinction. My previous article focused largely on the allegorical aspect of the Christian fairy-tale genre. However, allegory is an independent aspect of those works. As MacDonald says, "A fairytale is not [necessarily] an allegory. There may be allegory in it, but it is not an allegory." A fairy tale may lack specific allegorical symbolism—for example, Christ-figures in the form of lions and such—and may simply be an imaginative story that describes and draws us into another "realm", as my symphony's title calls it.

While stories from this realm may not always line up allegorically with a particular narrative, they may still be a great vehicle for beauty, truth, and goodness. MacDonald says a fairy tale "cannot help but have some meaning; if it have proportion and harmony, it has vitality, and vitality is truth. The beauty may be plainer in it than the truth, but without the truth the beauty could not be, and the fairytale would have no delight." He goes on to say that the realm

[1] George MacDonald, preface to *The Light Princess, and Other Fairy Tales* (New York: G. P. Putnam's Sons, 1893), http://www.george-macdonald.com/etexts/fantastic_imagination.html.

of Faerie is governed by the truth of its own consistent set of rules, which is perhaps also to say, its own consistent cultural milieu. For example, he says it would break the spell if we found "one of the gracious creatures of some childlike region talking Cockney." It may be noted here that many of our postmodern, so-called fairy-tale films like *Shrek*, *Tangled*, *Frozen*, *The Princess and the Frog*, *Ella Enchanted*, and *Enchanted* badly fail this test by constantly referring to modern pop culture (e.g., someone wisecracking that the monster "needs a Tic Tac" for his breath).

Likewise, in some seemingly abstract art, especially music, the transcendental value of "truth" may have to do with a consistent operating principle or musical language, perhaps unique to that composition. G. K. Chesterton said, "Art consists of limitation .... The most beautiful part of every picture is the frame."[2] Like a fairy tale, each piece of music (ideally) is framed by its own operational "rules", in terms of its particular style of melody, harmony, rhythm, and form. If you threw a few bars of Mozart into a composition by Wagner, the rules that govern the "realm" of Wagner would be broken. The world of the fairy tale in literature delights us with its "fantastic imagination" (MacDonald's phrase)—for example, talking animals in Narnia—because we understand Narnia's boundaries and its rules. Indeed, it would be more surprising to come across an animal in Narnia who could not speak.

For MacDonald, truth comes from "proportion and harmony", which create "vitality". Proportion in a musical composition has to do with, among other things, its form, the literal sense of proportion in time. For example,

[2] "The Toy Theatre", in G. K. Chesterton, *Tremendous Trifles* (New York: Dodd, Mead & Co., 1909), 182–83.

in a ternary form with an ABA design, we feel the music divided into thirds. The first melody (A) might go on for two minutes, and then a contrasting, new melody (B) might last the next two minutes, before A returns to balance the tripartite proportion for the last two minutes. Popular songs have something like this kind of plan in their arrangement of the verses and the choruses. Mac-Donald's use of the word *harmony* is metaphorical, not directly musical, as in "a harmonious arrangement of furniture in this room"—that is to say, a pleasing one. As a nineteenth-century writer, he could not have meant to include the discordant harmonies of twentieth-century Modernist music but was saying that vitality, ergo truth, is the product of pleasing (harmonious) sounds in discernible proportions.

MacDonald qualifies this idea of making up one's own set of rules by stating that the moral laws of our world are the exception, lest truth fundamentally be violated. This is to say that in a fairy tale we can change the rules of nature all we want, with flying elephants and talking giraffes, but we cannot create a fictional world where lying, stealing, and murder are perfectly acceptable: "The laws of the spirit of man must hold, alike in this world and in any world [man] may invent." Is this true of music, though? Are not abstract sounds in the air free from the imposition of moral law? I would reply that they are not free of an obligation to truth. If, in MacDonald's terms, you cannot hear in a certain piece anything like "proportion and harmony", then you are essentially hearing an attempted fairy tale whose enchantment has been broken by a fundamental violation of truth. He adds, "If my drawing, on the other hand, is so far from being a work of art that it needs THIS IS A HORSE written under it, what can it matter that neither you or your child can know what it means?" I have heard some pieces of music that need "THIS IS A HORSE" (or more to the point, "THIS IS MUSIC") written under them.

MacDonald further says, "A genuine work of art must mean many things; the truer its art, the more things it will mean." This certainly applies to music. Here is where he compares the fairy tale to a sonata. "If two or three men sat down to write each what the sonata meant to him, what approximation to definite idea would be the result? Little enough.... To one the sonata is a world of odour and beauty, to another of soothing only and sweetness." And here is his main point: "The greatest forces lie in the region of the uncomprehended." Music has a natural advantage here, being innately ineffable, whereas the presumption of words is that they are precise in nature. However, words can be woven into such fantastic imaginings that in their cumulative disposition, each word adding to the meaning of the previous ones, they can also possess transcendence, that is, "odour and beauty". To write and to read a fairy tale, he says, is not "to give [the reader] things to think about" but "to wake things up that are in him". Likewise, he says, "The best way with music, I imagine, is not to bring the forces of our intellect to bear upon it, but to be still and let it work on that part of us for whose sake it exists. We spoil countless things by intellectual greed." I am reminded of the words of Leonard Bernstein: "The most beautiful experience we can have is the mysterious [said Einstein]. Then why do so many of us constantly try to explain the beauty of music, thus apparently depriving it of its mystery?"[3]

This makes a good segue, to borrow a musical term, into a few comments on this new second movement of my

[3] Leonard Bernstein, *The Unanswered Question: Six Talks Given at Harvard* (Cambridge, Mass.: Harvard University Press, 1976), 9.

symphony. In the light of the above comments, I will say that in this movement, as in the first, I paid careful attention to "proportion" in the form and to a "harmonious" sound, generally. There are clear "fictional characters" in the form of different themes, but they will mean different things to different listeners, and, I hope, "wake things up" that are in them. There are allegories too, for me, as I described in part 1, but these remain private, and it is for the listener to use his own fantastic imagination and be willing to enter a fantastic realm. At the time of this writing, this symphony is a work on its way to the concert hall with a live orchestra, where there will be no visual images accompanying the performance. On my website, however, as with the first movement, I added some images for fun, which you are invited to view or ignore, as you wish. There is also a very realistic-sounding virtual "mock-up", which is what we composers create nowadays to give to conductors and producers, to "demo" how the work will sound. So the site provides a sneak peek at the behind-the-scenes stages in the creation of a symphony for large orchestra, as well as videos of both movements. (Perhaps by the time someone reads this, the symphony will have more movements done and posted, or may have been performed live and released on recording, and so that version will be available.)